ILLEGAL ALIENS

Their Employment and Employers

Barry R. Chiswick

University of Illinois at Chicago

1988

W.E. UPJOHN INSTITUTE for Employment Research

Library of Congress Cataloging-in-Publication Data

Chiswick, Barry R.
   Illegal aliens : their employment and employers / Barry R.
Chiswick.
     p.   cm.
   Bibliography: p.
   Includes index.
   ISBN 0-88099-059-7.   ISBN 0-88099-058-9 (pbk.)
   1. Aliens, Illegal—Employment—United States.   I. W.E. Upjohn
Institute for Employment Research.   II. Title.
HD8081.A5C473 1988
331.6'2'0973—dc19   88-10062
                                                 CIP

THE INSTITUTE, a nonprofit research organization, was established on July
1, 1945. It is an activity of the W. E. Upjohn Unemployment Trustee Corporation, which was formed in 1932 to administer a fund set aside by the late
Dr. W. E. Upjohn for the purpose of carrying on "research into the causes
and effects of unemployment and measures for the alleviation of unemployment."

The facts presented in this study and the observations and viewpoints expressed are the sole responsibility of the author. They do not necessarily represent
positions of the W. E. Upjohn Institute for Employment Research.

Carmella

AUTHOR

Barry R. Chiswick has been research professor in the Department of Economics and the Survey Research Laboratory at the University of Illinois at Chicago (UIC) since 1978. He received his Ph.D. in Economics from Columbia University, has held appointments at U.C.L.A., Columbia University, Stanford University and the University of Chicago, and was a senior staff economist on the Council of Economic Advisers. He is currently head of the Department of Economics at UIC.

Professor Chiswick's primary research interests have focused on labor markets, and in particular, on the determinants of the skills workers bring to labor markets and the returns these skills receive. For the past decade, this interest has been applied to studies of immigrants and racial and ethnic minorities.

He has published numerous articles in the major professional journals. His books include *Income Inequality, Human Resource and Income Distribution, The Gateway: U.S. Immigration Issues and Policies,* and *The Dilemma of American Immigration.*

ACKNOWLEDGEMENTS

For the "concept" of a survey of the employers of illegal aliens to evolve into this book, three ingredients were required from others: encouragement, financial support, and human resources.

I am especially appreciative of the confidence shown in the project by Ellen Sehgal, then of the Employment and Training Administration, U.S. Department of Labor. Our many discussions about the survey methodology were invaluable. The financial support provided by the Employment and Training Administration for the pilot survey made it possible to demonstrate the feasibility of the methodology.

The support for the project exhibited by Michael Teitelbaum, project officer, and Albert Rees, president of the Sloan Foundation, was most helpful. The Sloan Foundation's grant provided the resources for conducting the survey, as well as for the preliminary data analysis. Additional resources for data analysis and preliminary drafts were provided by the Hoover Institution, Stanford University, and the Center for the Study of the Economy and the State, University of Chicago. The W. E. Upjohn Institute for Employment Research made possible the preparation and publication of this book.

A special word of thanks is due to A.D. Moyer, district director, and the staff of the Chicago District Office of the Immigration and Naturalization Service for their cooperation and access to their files. A large debt is owed to the establishments, which shall remain anonymous, that participated in the survey.

All of the stages of the survey, from designing the sample to the preparation of the data tape for analysis, were done in conjunction with my colleagues at the Survey Research Laboratory, University of Illinois. Francis Fullam (pilot survey), Johnny Blair (sampling), Elizabeth Eastman (project coordinator), Diane Binson (project coordinator and data reduction coordinator), and Mary Hirt (project assistant) played major roles in the development and implementation of the survey. Karen Corrigan developed the interviewer instruction material and supervised the carefully selected interviewers who showed the skeptics that employers would participate in a survey on a potentially sensitive topic. Research assistance from Robert Wood and Gabriel Martinez greatly facilitated the data analysis.

The Social Science Data Archive of the University of Illinois at Chicago has generously agreed to make the data file available to other users.

Various aspects of the survey methodology and the analysis have been presented in workshops and conferences. These include workshops at Harvard University, the University of California, San Diego, the University of Chicago and the University of Illinois at Chicago, and the annual meetings of the American Economic Association, American Statistical Association, Population Association of America, Midwest Economics Association and the Association for Public Opinion Research. Comments on the preliminary drafts from Gary S. Becker, Carmel U. Chiswick, Evelyn Lehrer, Paul W. Miller, Ellen Sehgal and Alfred Tella have been very helpful in increasing the rigor of the analysis and the clarity of the presentation.

In spite of the invaluable assistance from many quarters, I accept responsibility for any errors of omission or commision in the survey and the analysis.

CONTENTS

TABLES

1
Introduction

This book is an analysis of the illegal alien labor market. It develops and tests hypotheses about the characteristics of the employment of illegal aliens, such as wages, investments in job training, job mobility, and workplace and employer characteristics. It also analyzes the employers of illegal aliens and how they differ from other employers. The empirical analysis is largely based on a unique data file. Detailed demographic and labor market data were transcribed from a sample of Immigration and Naturalization Services (INS) apprehension reports on illegal aliens in the Chicago metropolitan area. This was followed by an extensive interview of businesses in the Chicago metropolitan area, of whom half were identified by the illegal aliens and half were randomly selected. As a result it was possible to link data on the characteristics of illegal aliens to the survey responses of their employers, creating a unique employee-employer data file. Furthermore, the double-blind methodology of the employer survey permits the analysis of the similarities and differences between employers known to have hired an illegal alien and randomly selected employers. No comparable data has ever been constructed for the systematic study of illegal aliens.

I. The Background

Illegal aliens are individuals whose *presence* in the United States is in violation of the law. Some become illegal aliens as a result of a surreptitious entry: that is, by entering the U.S. without a proper inspection of their documents by INS border officials. This is

1

referred to as "entry without inspection," and in INS parlance these aliens are called "EWIs." They form the vast majority of the annual flow, as well as the majority of the stock of illegal aliens residing in the U.S. Others become illegal aliens because they violate a condition of a lawfully permitted entry. "Visa abusers" include foreign students who work in violation of their visas, tourists who stay longer than is permitted, and "temporary workers" (e.g., seasonal farm workers) who either work in sectors not covered by their permits or who remain longer than is allowed. Less numerous are those who enter with fraudulently obtained documents, which may be outright counterfeit visas or doctored documents. And there are those seamen, tourists and airline personnel who literally "jump ship" to enter the United States.

For obvious reasons the exact number of illegal aliens cannot be estimated with precision. This is a population which seeks to hide its identity and to avoid contact with governmental authorities. A recent review of various studies that have attempted to use indirect techniques to estimate the size of the resident illegal alien population suggests that in 1980 there were between 3.5 and 6.0 million, about half of whom were Mexican nationals (Siegel, Passel and Robinson, 1981). The large illegal alien flows across the border since then, deteriorating economic conditions in Mexico, prospects for amnesty, and other factors suggest that the number has grown since 1980. Since most newly arrived illegal aliens are young adults who come in search of work, a disproportionate number are in the labor force. By 1986 there may have been as many as 4 million illegal alien workers, comprising about 4 percent of the U.S. labor force. Surely the presence of such a large and growing component of the population and the labor force must have far-reaching effects.

For the past decade, the Executive Branch and Congress have been concerned with controlling illegal immigration. Starting with the Domestic Council Committee on Illegal Aliens under President Ford, which issued its report in 1976, through the task forces and the Select Commission on Immigration and Refugee Policy (1981 report) created during the Carter administration, and the further study groups and Congressional hearings during the Reagan administration, illegal aliens have been a primary focus of political and media attention.[1]

A compromise legislative package on illegal aliens that had been under discussion for a decade included penalties against employers who knowingly hire illegal aliens (referred to as "employer sanctions"), amnesty (or legalization) for illegal aliens who could prove they were in the U.S. prior to a specified date, and increased resources for INS enforcement activities. Quite unexpectedly, in the closing days of the legislative session, Congress passed and the President signed the Immigration Reform and Control Act of 1986.[2] This is the most sweeping immigration legislation since the 1965 Amendments which abolished the "national origins" quota system. The 1986 Act included employer sanctions, amnesty for illegal aliens who have continuously resided in the U.S. since January 1, 1982, and promises of increased enforcement resources, as well as other less central provisions. The implementation of the employer sanctions and legalization provisions began in the first half of 1987, and it will be some time before it will be possible to ascertain their consequences. Over 2¼ million illegal aliens have received legal status under the various amnesty provisions in the 1986 legislation.

Rather than laying to rest the illegal alien issue, the 1986 Act is a public acknowledgment that past policies failed. There is considerable skepticism that the new policies will succeed. Amnesty, intended to wipe the slate clean, may encourage additional illegal migration in the expectation of fraudulently qualifying for amnesty under the current act, and in the expectation that there will be future amnesties. Employer sanctions may have little if any effectiveness because of the difficulty of enforcement, particularly in the face of the nation's abhorrence of a national identity card system. Skeptics suggest that the promised resources for the enforcement of employer sanctions and for INS border and interior enforcement activities are not likely to be forthcoming. Since the political process failed to provide INS with adequate resources in the past, there is no reason to believe meaningful enforcement resources will be provided in the future.

Furthermore, the skeptics argue, as long as there are such large differences in economic well-being between the U.S. and so many other countries—in particular, our southern neighbor Mexico—the incentive for illegal migration will continue. The most effective deterrent, additional penalties against the illegal aliens themselves, was not seriously considered in the debate over immigration reform. If anything, a contrary approach was taken—rewarding with legal status those who entered the U.S. illegally, while continuing to deny visas to millions of applicants who have obeyed U.S. immigration law.[3]

It is clear that the illegal alien issue has not been legislated away by the 1986 Act. It is also clear that there is still too little rigorous social science research for the development of a deeper understanding of the illegal alien labor market, which is a prerequisite to the development of effective public policy.

Research on the labor market activities of illegal aliens has been hampered by the virtual absence of systematic and reliable data. This is not surprising—illegal aliens have an incentive to avoid revealing their status to an interviewer or in a questionnaire. As a result, anthropological or ethnographic approaches have sometimes been used by investigators. This type of research is subject to many pitfalls, including the problems inherent in small samples, selective respondents, and respondents reporting what they think the investigator wishes to hear. Others have relied on censored or preselected samples of illegal aliens, such as those who return to their home villages (Cornelius, 1976, and Diez-Canedo, 1980), have applied for social welfare benefits (Van Arsdol et al., 1978), or have been apprehended (North and Houstoun, 1976). Yet with few exceptions, even these techniques have not generated adequate data for labor market analysis.

[handwritten marginal note: as long as there are large differences in economic well-being between US / Mex the incentive]

Alth ...h to date on the labor market oppor ...llegal aliens suggests that this topic is not ...David North and Marion Houstoun (197(...apprehended illegal aliens in 1975, dem ...al aliens would respond to survey inte ...bular form descriptive statistics on the lab ...ic characteristics of the aliens. Using th ...t has been shown (Chiswick, 1984) that e ...usefully be applied to the analysis of i ...tivities. Earnings in the U.S. were found ...i, labor market experience in the U.S., and labor mai... in the country of origin, and that Mexican illegal aliens earned less than those of Canadian and European origins. Using a sample of Mexican-origin women in California who reported their legal status, Simon and DeLey (1984) analyzed the demographic and labor market characteristics of female illegal aliens.

Several studies have attempted to address the issue of "exploitation," that is, whether illegal aliens have lower status jobs or get paid less than other workers (see, for example, the summary and analysis in Massey, 1987). The key to the answer appears to be: which "other workers?" Illegal aliens, particularly those from Mexico, have a lower occupational attainment and lower earnings than workers in general. However, the gap apparently disappears when they are compared to other immigrants (by country of origin) with the same level of schooling and labor market experience in the U.S. Illegal aliens do apparently make fewer investments specific to the U.S. labor market, presumably because they and their employers are aware of a potentially less permanent attachment to this country.

These studies, and others, suggest that there can be substantial increases in our knowledge from the current very low base.[4] The purpose of this project is to learn more about the labor market opportunities, role and impact of illegal aliens in urban areas of the

U.S. This is done through the analysis of data on apprehended illegal aliens and their employers in the Chicago metropolitan area labor market.

II. The Survey

A more complete analysis of illegal alien labor market behavior requires information on the characteristics of both the illegal aliens and their employers. Data on where, with whom, and under what circumstances illegal aliens work would be difficult to acquire from the illegal aliens. First, sampling illegal aliens is difficult; and even when they are identified, the administration of a lengthy questionnaire in a variety of languages other than English would require complex and costly survey procedures. Second, there are many characteristics of the employer that may not be known to a typical worker. These characteristics include the wage structure of the firm, percent unionized, hiring policies and practices, and on-the-job training opportunities. This information would be even less accurate if obtained from workers who are relatively new to the country, and hence are less familiar with the language and labor market institutions, and are likely to have fewer years of experience with their current employer.

It was therefore decided that an analysis of the labor market behavior of illegal aliens required data on the person's demographic characteristics to be derived from the alien as well as data on the workplace to be derived from the employer. It was concluded that the most cost-effective and statistically reliable method for obtaining these data would be through combining administrative records on the illegal aliens with a survey of their employers.

Whenever an illegal alien is apprehended by the Immigration and Naturalization Services (INS), a Record of Deportable Alien, referred to by its form number, I-213, is completed. The form includes questions on demographic characteristics (e.g., age, sex, marital status), on nationality and immigrant status (e.g., country of birth, nationality, date of entry, method and place of entry), and on the person's labor market experience (e.g., whether employed, salary, and the name and address of the current or most recent employer). The alien's identification of the employer was used to obtain a sample of employers of illegal aliens that could then be interviewed about the characteristics of the establishment and its employees. The matching of data on the alien's characteristics and the employer's characteristics generates a unique data file. A limitation of the methodology is that INS apprehensions may not constitute a random sample of the resident illegal alien population.

To understand the characteristics of the employers of illegal aliens, a benchmark is needed. It is not possible to determine which firms have *never* employed illegal aliens. As an alternative, randomly selected employers can serve as the basis of comparison. Hence, the employer survey consists of two sets of employers —those identified by apprehended illegal aliens on the I-213 and those randomly selected from directories of establishments but matched by industry to the illegal alien employers.

By combining the data on the I-213 with the employer's responses, it is possible to analyze the labor market adjustment of illegal aliens. For example, to what extent do the earnings of illegal aliens vary not only with their age and duration of residence in the U.S., but also with the wage structure of their employer, the size of the establishment, the degree of unionization, and the racial/ethnic composition of co-workers? In addition, it is possible to trace the variation in employer (workplace) characteristics by the nationality and duration of residence in the U.S. of the illegal alien. For example, to what extent do illegal aliens in the U.S. a longer period of time work in larger, more highly unionized establishments that provide more on-the-job training?

Furthermore, the sample permits comparing the characteristics of establishments known to have employed an illegal alien with randomly selected establishments in the same industry. It is therefore possible to determine systematic differences between these employers by analyzing a variety of variables, including degree of unionization, ethnic heterogeneity, skill level, wage structure, and on-the-job training opportunities, among other characteristics.

The Chicago metropolitan area was selected as the site for the survey because it has a large, diversified economy and a large illegal alien population from a wide range of countries of origin.[5] This permits an analysis of one type of variation of particular interest for the study of illegal aliens, differences in labor market characteristics and employer characteristics by country of origin. It is particularly important to be able to distinguish between those of Mexican and non-Mexican origin in studies of this labor market. By limiting the analysis to only one site, findings from the analysis are not confounded by systematic variations that may exist across sites. Since the survey methodology is not site-specific, the procedures could be replicated elsewhere.

III. Chapter Outline

Chapter 2 sets the stage for the discussion of the survey and the data analysis. Illegal aliens are defined and there is a discussion of the number and characteristics of illegal aliens in the U.S. and Illinois. Since illegal immigration can only be understood as a result of the lack of concordance between the incentives for migrating *and the provisions for lawful migration, both issues are discussed.*

The survey methodology is presented in chapter 3. It includes the unique sampling plan and the interviewing procedures.[6] This is followed by an analysis of the effectiveness of the overall survey design and particular features of the survey.

The illegal alien is treated as the unit of observation in chapter 4. In addition to presentation of descriptive statistics, multiple regression analyses are reported for the wages of the illegal aliens. The wage rate analyses take advantage of the unique data features and analyze, in addition to the usual demographic and skill variables (such as marital status, labor market experience and country of origin), the relation between employer characteristics and wages. This is followed by an analysis of how the characteristics of the employers of illegal aliens vary by the country of origin and duration of U.S. residence of the aliens. Insights from the data analysis for this study, as well as other studies, are explored in the discussion of employer "exploitation" of illegal aliens.

The establishments become the unit of observation in chapter 5. The chapter begins with the some general descriptive statistics. It then develops and tests a model of the differences between employers of illegal aliens and randomly selected employers. An attempt is made to study the "underground economy" through an analysis of the differences between the two sets of employers. On-the-job training, another key issue in the discussion of illegal alien labor markets, is analyzed to test for differences between the two samples of employers. Finally, there is an analysis of employer differences in their understanding of their legal liabilities in the hiring of workers. Particular attention is given to their perception, or more accurately nonperception, regarding hiring foreign-born workers in general, and illegal aliens in particular.

This study closes in chapter 6 with a summary of the major findings, a synthesis of their implications, and an analysis of the likely effectiveness of the Immigration Reform and Control Act of 1986.

NOTES

[1] My own involvement with illegal alien research and policy began in 1975 when then-Attorney General Edward Levi, who was also chairman of the Domestic Council Committee on Illegal Aliens, asked the Council of Economic Advisers to provide technical assistance to the committee. As the CEA's Senior Staff Economist in human resources I was assigned to the task. I quickly discovered that very little was known about illegal aliens, or even immigrants in general. In part because of the clandestine nature of the illegal alien population and limited research resources, the increase in knowledge about illegal aliens over the decade has been quite small.

[2] The Act can be found in U.S. House of Representatives (1986). For an analysis of the provisions and likely consequences of the 1986 Act see Chiswick (1988).

[3] Although most applicants for legalization will have to demonstrate they have resided "continuously" in the U.S. for at least five years, less stringent provisions apply for seasonal farm workers. Under special provisions in the 1986 Act, seasonal agricultural workers (SAWs) may be granted amnesty if they worked in U.S. perishable crop agriculture for at least 90 days in 1986. About one-fifth of those granted amnesty applied under the SAW provisions.

[4] Other studies of illegal aliens that are relevant for understanding their decision to migrate illegally, their adjustment in the U.S., and their impact include Bustamante (1977), Cross and Sandos (1981), Davidson (1981), Cardenas (1979), Huddle, Corwin and MacDonald (1985), Papandemetriou and DiMarzio (1986); Piore (1979), Portes (1977), Van Arsdol et al. (1978). See also the special issue of the *International Migration Review,* entitled *Irregular Migration: An International Perspective* (Fall 1984).

[5] The classic analysis of employer-based urban labor market data also used Chicago as the survey site. See Rees and Shultz (1970).

[6] For a more detailed discussion see Chiswick (1985, Volume I, chapters 2 and 3). The I-213 abstract form, establishment questionnaire, interviewer training manual and other documents for the survey are reproduced in Chiswick (1985, Volume II).

2

Immigration Policy and Illegal Aliens

This chapter is concerned with setting the stage for the survey and analysis presented in subsequent chapters. Illegal aliens are defined in section I. Because illegal migration can be understood only in the context of legal immigration, section II presents a summary of current immigration law. This is followed (section III) by an analysis of the implications of a divergence between the incentives for migrating and the legal migration permitted under current law. Not all unsuccessful visa applicants become illegal aliens. Three selection processes are involved—a desire to migrate, an inability to obtain a visa, and the decision to migrate illegally. Implications of these selection processes for the characteristics and labor market behavior of illegal aliens are developed.

I. Who Are the Illegal Aliens?

Illegal aliens are foreign nationals whose mere presence in the United States is in violation of the law or who have violated a condition of a legal entry into the country. Persons who entered the United States illegally include those who avoided a border inspection of their international travel documents. This is referred to as "entry without inspection," and these illegal aliens are referred to in INS parlance as "EWIs." The stereotypical EWI would be a Mexican illegal alien who surreptitiously crossed the border at night.

Illegal immigrants also include those who gained entry through the use of fraudulent documents, such as a counterfeit visa or

11

passport, or a fraudulent visa application. This category gained recent attention from the denaturalization (i.e., rescinding the granting of citizenship) and deportation of aliens who had fraudulently indicated that they had not participated in World War II Nazi war-crimes when they applied for entry into the U.S.

Those who "abuse" or violate the conditions of a lawfully obtained visa are also illegal aliens. Visa abusers include foreign nationals who have remained longer than the time span permitted by their tourist, student, guest worker or other type of temporary visa or papers that permitted their lawful entry into the U.S. It also includes those who violate a condition of their visa, such as working in violation of a student or tourist visa.

Illegal aliens exist because the desires of some to be in the United States for employment or other purposes come into conflict with U.S. efforts to regulate who may enter and remain in this country, and under what terms or conditions. Illegal immigration also exists because of the imperfect enforcement of immigration law. Illegal immigration would end if all attempts at illegal entry or violating a condition of a legal entry resulted with perfect certainty in an instantaneous apprehension and deportation.

It is not surprising that illegal immigration became an important policy issue only after the U.S. imposed a quantitative restriction on immigration. The first major source country of illegal immigration was China because the first quantitative immigration barriers introduced by the U.S. were against Chinese laborers, starting with legislation in 1875 banning the immigration of Asian contract laborers. Over the past century, as the immigration law has changed and there have been shifts in the source countries of those desiring to immigrate, the composition of illegal aliens has also changed.

The various categories of illegal aliens are not equally represented in the illegal alien population. In INS terminology, apprehended illegal aliens are referred to as "deportable aliens located." Nearly all "deportable aliens located" accept a "voluntary departure," that is, they voluntarily agree to leave the U.S. Some aliens petition to remain and therefore require a deportation hearing. Some will be successful. For example, an illegal alien who is the spouse of a U.S. citizen, where the marriage is deemed to be *bona fide,* can expect to receive an "adjustment of status," that is, to receive a resident alien visa. For others, however, the end of the process is a formal deportation. In fiscal year 1984, the year in which the employer survey was conducted, over 1.2 million deportable aliens were located, and over 930,000 aliens were expelled, but there were only 18,000 formal deportations (*Statistical Yearbook,* 1986, p. 188).

Of the more than 1.2 million deportable aliens located in fiscal year 1984, a rather typical recent year, 96 percent had entered the U.S. without inspection (EWIs) (see table 2-1). Mexican nationals, who were apprehended EWIs comprised 96.9 percent of all EWI apprehensions, or 93.0 percent of all apprehensions of illegal aliens. Most of the EWIs are apprehended within hours, if not minutes, of entering the U.S. from Mexico, and are returned to the other side of the border within a day.

Among the 50,624 non-EWI illegal alien apprehensions in 1984, 61 percent had violated a visitor visa and 12 percent had violated a student visa, primarily by working or staying longer than the visa allowed. Another 10 percent were crewmen of ships and aircraft who "jumped ship," and for the remaining 17 percent, a host of other reasons resulted in their illegal status. Among Eastern Hemispheric illegal aliens—from Europe, Asia and Africa—the "abuse" of a visitor or student visa or jumping ship were the primary reasons for an illegal status. Illegal migration is that much more difficult when a valid visa (tourist or student) is needed to enter the U.S., rather than merely walking across the border.

While the long, thinly guarded border with Mexico facilitates uninspected illegal border crossings, it is not sufficient to explain the large numbers of Mexican nationals among the illegal alien population. The border with Canada is longer and less well guarded. Yet, of the 6,924 Canadian illegal aliens apprehended in 1984, almost as many had violated a visitor visa (2,985) as had entered without

Table 2-1
Deportable Aliens Located by Status at Entry and Nationality, 1984 Fiscal Year

Nationality	Entry without inspection	Visitor	Student	Crewman	Other	Total	Percent of total
Europe	667	4,034	783	742	602	6,828	0.5
Asia	702	3,987	1,814	2,427	1,001	9,931	0.8
North America	1,190,095	15,691	1,214	901	5,491	1,213,392	97.3
Mexico	1,159,101	8,194	373	173	2,928	1,170,769	93.9
South America	3,939	3,887	627	427	1,025	9,905	0.8
Africa	69	1,543	1,168	208	176	3,164	0.3
Other	881	1,587	647	220	422	3,757	0.3
Total	1,196,353	30,729	6,253	4,925	8,717	1,246,977	100.0
Percent of Total	95.9	2.5	0.5	0.4	0.7	100.0	

SOURCE: U.S. Department of Justice, *1984 Statistical Yearbook of the Immigration and Naturalization Service*, Washington: U.S. Government Printing Office, 1986, Table ENF 1.2, p. 189.

inspection (3,285). Nor does U.S. immigration law grant more legal resident alien visas to Canadian than Mexican nationals. In fiscal year 1984, more than 57,500 Mexican nationals immigrated legally to the U.S., compared to less than 10,800 Canadians.

Easy access may be a necessary condition for widescale attempts at illegal entry, but is not a sufficient reason. Differences in economic opportunities are a key element in the immigration story. The number of apprehensions of nationals per 1,000 population in the country of origin was about 11.5 for Mexican nationals and 0.3 for Canadians. While the gap in economic well-being and consumption between the U.S. and Canada is small, the gap between the U.S. and Mexico is very large (table 2-2). The GNP per capita in the U.S. is measured to be about 15 percent greater than in Canada, a difference that is quite small relative to the measurement problems and the costs of migration. However, the U.S. per capita GNP was about four times the Mexican magnitude. Compared with the U.S. or Canada, infant mortality rates are six times higher in Mexico, the population per physician ratio is four times higher, and the number of persons per automobile is seven times higher. Furthermore, in spite of a rapidly declining fertility rate, the rate of growth of the Mexican population is 2 1/2 times the U.S. and Canadian growth rates. The divergence in natural rates of increase in the population is even greater since the U.S. and Canadian population growth is enhanced by substantial net immigration.

Data on country differences in income or consumption per capita may not properly reflect opportunities for the same person in each of the two countries. Data are generally not available on the income or consumption of immigrants pre-and postmigration. One exception is the North-Houstoun (1976) survey of apprehended illegal aliens who in 1975 were asked whether they had in their home in their country of origin and in the U.S. electricity, running water, and a TV or radio. Of the more than 400 Mexican illegal aliens who responded to the question, 39 percent did not have running water in Mexico, but only 5 percent did not have it in the U.S. For electricity, 26 percent did not have it in Mexico, but only 2 percent

Table 2-2
Selected Measures of Economic Well-being,
U.S., Canada, Mexico[a]

Item	U.S.	Canada	Mexico
Population (1984) (millions)	236.7	25.1	77.7
Percent Change in Population (annual rate 1980-84)	1.0	1.1	2.6
GNP per Capita (U.S. $, 1982)	$12,482	$10,610	$3,114
Infant Mortality (per 1,000 live births)	11	10	61
Population per Physician	549	548	2,136
Public Expenditure for Education as Percent of GNP	6.9	7.7	3.9
Persons per Car	1.8	2.3	14.0
Telephones per 1,000 Pop.	79	69	8
TV Sets per 1,000 Pop.	631	489	111

a. Data refer to years 1980-82 unless noted otherwise.

SOURCE: U.S. Bureau of the Census, *Statistical Abstract of the United States, 1985,* 105th Edition, Washington, D.C.: U.S. Government Printing Office, 1986, Tables 1475, 1478, 1480, 1481, 1486, and 1487.

did not have it in the U.S. A more mixed picture emerges for a TV or radio. Of those who had a TV or radio in Mexico, nearly 80 percent had one or more in the U.S., while two-thirds of those without a TV or radio in Mexico had one or more in the U.S. Thus, these crude indices of consumption imply substantial improvements in levels of real economic well-being even for fairly recent illegal aliens.[1]

Another study estimated the net economic gain from working in the U.S. for a sample of Mexican aliens employed in the fall 1978 Hood River Valley (Oregon) apple harvest (Cuthbert and Stevens, 1981). The workers were young (average age 27 years), with little schooling (4.4 years), primarily single (61 percent), disproportionately from the state of Jalisco (51 percent), recently entered the U.S., but had prior U.S. harvest experience (6 seasons). These characteristics were more intense (except for prior U.S. experience) for the 78 illegal aliens than for the 15 legal aliens in the sample. U.S. earnings during the harvest season were six times what the aliens reported they could have earned in Mexico. After deducting from U.S. earnings the costs of the migration (including payments to alien smugglers) and certain additional expenses for living in the U.S., Cuthbert and Stevens estimated net U.S. earnings to be three times what the migrants could have received in Mexico during the same work period.

There has been an increase in EWI apprehensions of Central and South American nationals who pass through Mexico on the way to the U.S. For example, of the 24,000 El Salvadorian and Guatemalan illegal aliens apprehended in 1984, 22,000 were EWIs. Because of the difficulties of gaining access to a land border, EWI entries from the Eastern Hemisphere are relatively rare.

Any portrait of apprehended illegal aliens is necessarily swamped by the preponderance in the data of EWIs, especially Mexican EWIs. For several reasons this presents a distorted picture of the illegal alien population residing in the U.S. One reason is the extent of multiple apprehensions of the same individual. An apprehended EWI returned across the Mexican border may merely try again the next night, and perhaps appear in the statistics once again! Another is that the low cost of crossing the Mexican border, compared to other forms of entry, may encourage far greater to and fro migration for Mexican nationals than for other nationals, thereby increasing the number of apprehensions. A visit home is more costly for a Korean illegal alien, not only because of the greater out-of-pocket expenses involved in the travel, but also because illegal entry is more difficult and a deportation more costly. Finally, the relatively low cost per apprehension to the INS when resources are placed on the Mexican border may have encouraged a greater emphasis on border enforcement.[2] This would increase the representation of Mexican EWIs in the apprehension data, and create exaggerated impressions as to their preponderance in the illegal alien population.

Although apprehensions of illegal aliens are easy to measure, these data reflect flows of individuals and INS enforcement policies, rather than the stock of illegal aliens residing in the U.S. It has been difficult to estimate the size and characteristics of the resident illegal alien population. This arises in part because there may be sharp seasonal, cyclical and secular changes in the net flow and hence the stock of illegal aliens . During the "on-season" (the spring , summer and early fall), during peaks in the U.S. business cycle when the economy is closer to full employment, and during periods of economic distress in the sending countries (in particular Mexico), more illegal aliens enter and fewer leave. It is always difficult to measure the size and characteristics of a fluid population.

More important, however, is the obvious incentive of illegal aliens to avoid revealing their immigration status in an administrative record, a survey or a census. There is no gain to the individual from being candid about his or her illegal status, and there is always some possibility that revealing the information will result in some "cost," such as deportation or the loss of income transfer benefits. Indeed, illegal aliens may attempt to avoid revealing even their presence or existence to an interviewer or enumerator to reduce the probability of deportation. As a result, direct survey research techniques cannot be used to study the illegal alien population.

Several studies have attempted to use indirect procedures to estimate the number of illegal aliens in the U.S. These methodologies generally involve three steps. The first step is the estimation of the legal resident population (citizen and resident aliens) at a point in time. The second step is to "age" that population to a later point in time. The third step is to take the difference between the "aged" population and the estimated total population in the later time period. The difference is the estimated number of illegal aliens. A major limitation of this methodology is that each statistic, the estimated legal population and the estimated total population, is measured with error. The difference between two large numbers, each of which is estimated with independent random error, is a number with substantial measurement error.[3]

Nonetheless, the studies that have attempted to measure the stock of the illegal alien population are instructive. After reviewing the methodology in several studies, three Census Bureau statisticians (Siegel, Passel and Robinson, 1981) concluded:

> The total number of illegal residents in the United States in some recent year, say 1978, is almost certainly below 6.0 million, and may be substantially less, possibly only 3.5 to 5.0 million. . . . The Mexican component of the illegally resident population is almost certainly less than 3.0 million and may be substantially less, possibly only 1.5 to 2.5 million. The gross movement into the United States of Mexican illegals is considerable, as is reflected in the large numbers of apprehensions made by INS, but this "immigration" is largely offset by a considerable movement in the opposite direction.

In a more recent study, Passel and Woodrow (1984) estimated the number and characteristics of illegal aliens enumerated in the 1980 Census of Population. They estimated a total of 2.1 million illegal aliens, of whom about 55 percent are Mexican nationals. While the Passel and Woodrow estimates are lower than those reported by Siegel, Passel, and Robinson, a substantial underenumeration of illegal aliens in the census is to be expected. If one-third or one-half of the actual number of resident illegal aliens avoided enumeration, the Passel and Woodrow estimates would imply 3.1 to 4.2 million illegal aliens. Passel and Woodrow also estimated the number of illegal aliens by state and within states by certain demographic characteristics. The precision of these estimates necessarily diminishes with a smaller degree of aggregation.

Since the survey and data analysis in the following chapters refer to the Chicago SMSA and since most illegal aliens who reside in

Illinois are believed to live in the Chicago SMSA, the Passel and
Woodrow estimates for Illinois are particularly relevant. Table 2-3
compares the data on Illinois with the U.S. as a whole. The
estimated 135,000 illegal aliens in Illinois is 6.6 percent of the
estimated total resident illegal alien population. The distribution by
period of entry and age are very similar in Illinois and for the
country as a whole. About 45 percent of the illegal aliens arrived
during 1975-80, 30 percent during 1970-74, and 25 percent before
1970.[4] By age, almost two-thirds were 15 to 34 years old in 1980,
with just under 20 percent less than age 15 and another 20 percent
age 35 or older. There are somewhat greater differences by country
of origin. It is estimated that 75 percent of the Illinois illegal aliens
are from Mexico, compared with 55 percent nationwide. On the
other hand, Illinois has relatively fewer illegal aliens from other
Western Hemispheric countries. The proportions of Eastern Hemisphere illegal aliens are, 16.1 percent for Illinois and 21.9 percent
nationwide. Thus, the Passel and Woodrow estimates suggest that
illegal aliens in Illinois have demographic characteristics very
similar to those of illegal aliens nationwide. The primary difference,
if any, is a greater proportion of Mexican nationals and a lesser
proportion of other Western Hemispheric illegal aliens in Illinois.

II. Current Immigration Law

An appreciation of the issues involved in illegal immigration can
be obtained only within the context of the legal avenues for
immigration. Illegal immigration, whether permanent or temporary, may, but need not, arise when opportunities for legal immigration are closed.

Current immigration law has its basis in the 1965 Amendments to
the 1952 Immigration and Nationality Act. The 1952 Act was
largely a recodification of existing law. The 1965 Amendments
liberalized immigration restrictions facing eastern and southern
Europe and Asia, but was restrictive with regards to northwestern
Europe and the Western Hemisphere. The 1965 Amendments

Table 2-3

Estimated Number and Characteristics of Illegal Aliens Enumerated in the 1980 Census for the U.S. and Illinois

(Numbers in thousands)

Item		Illinois		U.S.	
		Number	Percent[a]	Number	Percent[a]
All illegal aliens					
Number		135	100.0	2,057	100.0
Period of entry:	1975-80	61	45.2	941	45.7
	1970-74	43	31.9	576	28.0
	Before 1970	32	23.7	540	26.3
Country of	Mexico	101	74.8	1,131	55.0
origin:	Other W. Hem.	12	8.9	477	23.2
	Europe	9	6.7	150	7.3
	Asia	10	7.4	213	10.4
	Other	3	2.0	86	4.2
Age:	Under 15	—	16.0	—	18.1
	15-34 years	—	64.7	—	62.2
	35 years & older	—	19.3	—	17.8
Sex ratio	Under 15	—	50.7	—	—
(percent male)	15-34 years	—	58.8	—	51.7
by age:	35 years & older	—	56.7	—	55.4
	All ages	—	57.3	—	53.3
Mexican illegal aliens					
Age:	Under 15	—	17.8	—	21.3
	15-34 years	—	64.2	—	63.0
	35 years & older	—	18.0	—	15.7
Sex ratio	Under 15	—	50.5	—	50.5
(percent male)	15-34 years	—	60.8	—	57.4
by age:	35 years & older	—	57.8	—	50.2
	All ages	—	58.3	—	55.0

SOURCE: Jeffrey S. Passel and Karen A. Woodrow "Geographic Distribution of Undocumented Immigrants: Estimates of Undocumented Aliens Counted in the 1980 Census by State," *International Migration Review.* Vol 18 (3), Fall 1984, pp. 642-671.

NOTE: — designates the data not reported in the source.

a. With the exception of the sex ratio, for each category the sum of the entries totals to 100 percent, except for rounding.

abolished the pernicious "national origins" quota system. The national origins quota system had been instituted in the 1920s to severely restrict eastern and southern European immigration. Asian immigration, which had been limited by late 19th and early 20th century legislation and administrative action, had been barred in the 1917 immigration law. The 1965 Amendments also reduced the emphasis, introduced in the 1952 legislation, on skill or occupation for rationing visas among applicants from within a country.

The 1965 Amendments introduced numerical limits on Western Hemispheric immigration. It also introduced a system of "preferences" with a heavy emphasis on kinship with a U.S. citizen or resident alien as the rationing mechanism. Skill and refugee status were given relatively minor roles.

The basic features of current immigration law, including the changes introduced by the Refugee Act of 1980 and other amendments, are outlined in table 2-4. The number of immigrants "admitted" to the United States under various categories is shown in table 2-5 for 1984. The worldwide, country and preference category quotas indicated in table 2-4 refer to ceilings on the number of visas issued in a year. The data on immigration refer to the number of persons entering the United States with an immigrant visa or receiving a change in status to permanent resident alien. Immigrant visas need not be used in the fiscal year they are issued, and some are never used.

A person can receive immigrant status (permanent resident alien status) under one of four general categories—as an immediate relative of a U.S. citizen, by other kinship criteria, by occupation (skill), and through refugee status. In addition, refugees can be given asylum or parole status by the U.S. Attorney General, which enables them to enter and work in the United States indefinitely, although most eventually obtain an adjustment of status and become permanent resident aliens.

The immediate relatives of U.S. citizens, that is, the spouse, unmarried minor children, and parents of adult citizens, can enter

Table 2-4

Summary of the Immigration Law Under the 1965 Amendments to the Immigration and Nationality Act and Subsequent Amendments

Immigrants not subject to numerical limitation

A. Spouse and minor children of U.S. citizens and the parents of U.S. citizens over age 21

B. Refugees and Asylees (Since the Refugee Act of 1980)

Immigrants subject to numerical limitation in the preference system

	Quotas (visas per year)		
	1965-1978	1978-1980	1981-present
?re[a]	170,000 }	290,000	270,000
.iere[a]	120,000 }		
	20,000	20,000	20,000

Preference system[c]

	nmarried adult children ' U.S. citizens	20 percent
	pouse and unmarried :hildren of permanent esident aliens	20 percent (26 percent), plus any not required for first preference[d]
Third	Professionals, scientists, and artists of exceptional ability	10 percent
Fourth	Married children of U.S. citizens	10 percent plus any not required for first three preferences
Fifth	Siblings of U.S. citizens	24 percent plus any not required for first four preferences
Sixth	Workers in occupations for which labor is scarce in the U.S.	10 percent

Preference system[c]

Seventh[e]	Refugees[e]	6 percent[e]
Nonpre-ference[f]	Any applicant not entitled to a preference	Numbers not required for preference applicants
	Spouse and minor children of any preference applicant can be classified with the same preference if a visa is not otherwise available	Charged to appropriate preference

SOURCE: Immigration and Naturalization Service.

a. The hemisphere quotas were converted to a combined world ceiling of 290,000 visas by the 1978 Amendments and reduced to 270,000 visas per year when the Refugee Act of 1980 removed refugees from the preference system.

b. Country Ceiling applicable to the Eastern Hemisphere under the 1965 Amendments and the Western Hemisphere since the 1977 amendments.

c. Preference system applicable to the Eastern Hemisphere under the 1965 Amendments and the Western Hemisphere under the 1977 Amendments. Prior to 1977, Western Hemisphere visas issued on a first-come, first-served basis. Within the country ceiling, colonies or dependencies had a ceiling of 600 visas, which was raised to 5,000 visas in the 1986 amendments.

d. Increased from 20 percent of 290,000 visas to 26 percent of the 270,000 visas with the passage of the Refugee Act of 1980.

e. The Refugee Act of 1980 established a temporary annual quota of 50,000 visas for refugees outside of the preference system and gave the President authority to admit additional refugees and to admit refugees indefinitely after the expiration of the temporary provisions. The refugee quota is now set annually. The 1980 Act changed the definitions of "refugee" to a person with a well-founded fear of religious, political, or racial persecution regardless of country or origin, whereas refugee status was previously applicable only to persons fleeing a Communist country or the general area of the Middle East.

f. Nonpreference applicants have to obtain a labor certificate (i.e. demonstrate they have a "needed" skill and a job waiting for them), invest money in a business in the U.S., or satisfy some other criterion to demonstrate their economic value to the U.S. immigration of the spouses and children of U.S. citizens and only secondarily because of the increased immigration of parents.

the United States without numerical limitation. Although the number of persons entering the United States in this manner had fluctuated around 100,000 annually in the decade after 1965, it increased to over 150,000 annually in 1980, and is now approxi-

Table 2-5
Immigrants Admitted to the U.S. by Class of Admission, 1984[a]

Category	Number	Percent
Exempt from numerical limit	**281,887**	**51.8**
Immediate relatives of U.S. citizens	177,783	32.7
Refugee and asylee adjustments	92,127	16.9
Other[b]	11,977	2.2
Subject to limit (preferences system)	**262,016**	**48.2**
First (unmarried children of U.S. citizens)	7,569	1.4
Second (spouses and unmarried children of resident aliens)	112,309	20.6
Third (professionals or highly skilled workers)[c]	24,852	4.6
Fourth (married children of U.S. citizens)	14,681	2.7
Fifth (siblings of U.S. citizens)	77,765	14.3
Sixth (needed skilled or unskilled workers)[c]	24,669	4.5
Nonpreference	0	0.0
Other special visas	171	0.0
Total	**543,903**	**100.00**

SOURCE: U.S. Department of Justice, *1984 Statistical Yearbook of the Immigration and Naturalization Service,* Washington: U.S. Government Printing Office, 1986, Table IMM 1.5, p. 11-14.

a. Spouses and children of visa recipients included in totals.

b. Includes ministers (1,540), spouses of U.S. citizens who entered as fiance(e)s (5,464), children born abroad to resident aliens (3,639) and other special categories.

c. Includes 10,691 third preference and 11,393 sixth preference "principals" (i.e., recipients of labor certifications). The remainder are spouses and children.

mately 200,000 per year. This has been largely due to the increased immigration of the spouses and children of U.S. citizens and only secondarily because of the increased immigration of parents.

Western Hemisphere immigrant visas subject to numerical limit had been rationed on a first-come first-served basis under the 1965 Amendments. Legislation enacted in 1977 brought them under the same rationing system as the Eastern Hemisphere. This rationing system is largely based on kinship. Currently 80 percent of the annual number of 270,00 numerically limited visas are reserved for the adult children (first and fourth preferences) and siblings (fifth preference) of U.S. citizens, and the spouse and unmarried children of permanent resident aliens (second preference). The spouse and minor children of any person receiving a visa can generally receive a visa in the same preference category if a visa is not otherwise available for them.

The two remaining preferences, the third and sixth, are for persons who can demonstrate a U.S. labor market "need" for their services. The third preference is for professionals of exceptional ability (professors, scientists, artists, etc.), while the sixth is for skilled workers in occupations with a scarce U.S. labor supply (e.g., chefs). A labor certificate, issued by the Office of Labor Certification in the U.S. Department of Labor, is a prerequisite for an occupational preference visa. To obtain a labor certificate a U.S. employer must petition on behalf of the visa applicant and demonstrate that no appropriate worker can be found in the U.S. at the "prevailing wage." Although it would seem that 20 percent of the preference visa applicants are to some extent "skill" tested, more than half of the 3rd and 5th preference visa recipients are the spouses and minor children of labor certification recipients (see table 2-5).

Of the more than 540,000 immigrants "admitted" to the U.S. in 1984, about 345,000 were new arrivals and nearly 200,000 received an adjustment of their status to that of an immigrant (primarily, refugees and relatives of U.S. citizens). Nearly two-thirds of the immigrants were admitted under kinship criteria, one-quarter under refugee criteria, and less than 10 percent under the occupational preferences (of whom half are the relatives of occupational preference principals).

Current law includes a country limit of 20, 000 visas per year, but only for visas subject to numerical limit.[5] While there are some slight differences between country of birth and country of "chargeability" under immigration law, they are largely one and the same.

The countries for which this ceiling tends to be most binding include China, India, Korea, the Philippines and Mexico. Immigration from these countries can be substantially in excess of the 20,000 level as a result of the absence of a limit on the immediate relatives of U.S. citizens. Among 1984 immigrants born in Mexico, for example, about one-third were subject to the ceiling (19,576), while nearly two-thirds were exempt, largely because they were the immediate relatives of U.S. citizens (table 2-6). Only one-tenth of 1 percent of Mexican immigrants were "skill tested" as occupational preference principals.

Table 2-6

Immigrants Born in Mexico Admitted to the U.S. by Category, 1984

Category	Number	Percent
Exempt from numerical limit	**37,981**	**66.0**
Immediate relatives of U.S. citizens[a]	35,785	62.2
Children born aboard to resident aliens	2,003	3.5
Other	193	0.3
Subject to limit (preferences)	**19,576**	**34.0**
Relative preferences	19,291	33.5
Occupational preferences—principals	62	0.1
Occupational preferences—relatives	174	0.3
Other	49	0.1
Total	**57,557**	**100.0**

SOURCE: U.S. Department of Justice, *1984 Statistical Yearbook of the Immigration and Naturalization Service,* Washington: U.S. Government Printing Office, 1986, Tables IMM 2.3, IMM 2.6, IMM 3.1.

a. Parents, spouses, fiances and children of U.S. citizens.

The Immigration Reform and Control Act of 1986 did not introduce any major changes in the provisions for obtaining a permanent resident alien visa ("green card"), except for amnesty for illegal aliens and a new "replenishment agricultural worker" (RAW) program, (U.S. House of Representatives, 1986).[6] Under the 1986 Act, amnesty is generally to be granted to illegal aliens who have been in the U.S. "continuously" since before January 1, 1982. A twelve-month application period for the "temporary resident alien status" began in May 1987. After 18 months in this status, the aliens must apply for permanent resident alien status within a 12-month period or else lapse into an illegal status. Granting permanent resident alien status will be virtually automatic for the legalized aliens who apply and have some minimal understanding of English.

Different provisions apply for "special agricultural workers" (SAWs), that is, illegal aliens who have worked in perishable-crop agriculture in the U.S. for at least 90 days during the 12-month period ending May 1, 1986. They may apply for temporary resident alien status. Their period in the temporary resident alien category ranges from 12 to 24 months, varying inversely with the number of seasons they have worked in the U.S. seasonal agriculture.

The 1986 Act includes a ceiling of 350,000 permanent resident alien visas that may be granted under the agricultural worker program (SAW). Otherwise, there are no country or worldwide ceilings on the number of aliens eligible for amnesty, and legalized aliens are not counted against country or worldwide ceilings. Upon receipt of permanent resident alien status, those receiving amnesty may serve as immigration sponsors for relatives who are not already in the U.S.

The 1986 Act also provides for a three-year "replenishment agricultural worker" (RAW) program starting in fiscal year 1990, when the SAW temporary resident alien period comes to an end. To be activated, the Secretaries of Labor and Agriculture must determine that there is a "shortage" of workers who are qualified and available for seasonal farm work. Persons receiving temporary worker status under the RAW provision must work in perishable agriculture for at least 90 days in each of three consecutive years before becoming permanent resident aliens. After becoming permanent resident aliens, they must also work for at least five seasons in agriculture to be eligible for naturalization. Previous temporary farm workers programs, such as the *bracero* program (1942 to 1964) and the current H-2 program, have not provided opportunities for obtaining a permanent resident alien visa.

Although amnesty and the RAW program are one-time events under the provisions of the 1986 Act, it is reasonable to assume that as illegal immigration continues, they will become recurring events. In general, the 1986 Act is much more generous in providing labor for seasonal farm work than for other sectors of the economy.

The binding nature of U.S. immigration law means that only a subset of persons who would like to immigrate can do so readily. Obtaining a visa is easier if a potential applicant has relatives already in the U.S., and the ease is greater the more immediate the relationship and if the relative is a citizen. Obtaining a visa is more difficult if a larger number of nationals from one's country of origin also seek a visa and if a refugee status cannot be claimed.

The combined effects of large demand for immigrant visas from many countries of origin and a limited supply of visas result in a large pool of actual and potential unsuccessful visa applicants. The size of the pool cannot be measured directly. It is surely larger than the sum of the number of individuals who are in the visa "backlog" (or queue) waiting their turn and the number who have been denied a visa. Many individuals who wish to immigrate but who know they cannot qualify for a visa under current law would not even apply.

III. Incentives for Illegal Migration

As indicated above, there are three selection criteria relevant for determining who will be an illegal alien: the decision to migrate; the inability to obtain a lawful visa; and the decision to migrate in violation of the law.

Immigrants can be classified in several major categories. Economic migrants are those who move primarily on the basis of their estimate of their earning potential in the destination compared to that in the origin. For economic migrants, immigration can be viewed in terms of a human capital investment. A human capital investment is an expenditure of time and other resources that raises the labor market productivity embodied in a person. Although usually thought of in terms of schooling and on-the-job training, the definition applies equally well to migration. A change in the person's locale is clearly embodied in the person, and for economic migrants the primary objective is the greater real income from moving from where their skills are less well rewarded to where they are more highly rewarded.

Economic migrants tend to be unmarried young adults. With an increase in labor market experience in the origin there is an increase in skills that are useful in the origin, but which may have little transferability to a destination. This raises the cost of migrating (the value of the lost earnings during the migration process), as well as reduces the earnings differential between the origin and destination. There is also "location-specific" capital not directly related to the labor market. This includes information about and an attachment to the place of origin, including family and friends in the origin. The greater these attachments, the greater the cost of moving. Furthermore, a nonworking spouse and young children raise the cost of migrating without impacting on the benefit side of the scale.

Immigrants, and migrants in general, seem to have another characteristic that is not as easy to quantify. Immigrants are sometimes described as "favorably self-selected." That is, they are more able, ambitious, risk-taking and/or entrepreneurial individuals than those who remain in the origin. These characteristics are not surprising, they are the very characteristics that are likely to be associated with greater economic benefits in the higher income destination.[7]

Migrating across international borders involves much more than just the initial move. Most important is the adaptation to the new environment. Individuals who are more flexible and those who are better decisionmakers will be more successful immigrants. Hence economic migrants can be expected to have more "allocative skills," that is skills in making decisions by acquiring and combining diverse pieces of information.[8]

Tied movers are individuals whose migration decision is largely based on the migration behavior of another family member—a spouse, parent, child or sibling. Because their own economic incentives are less central, they are less likely to have the unique economic migrant profile—unmarried young adult with transferable skills and favorably self-selected, or labor market success.

Refugees are individuals who leave their origin not primarily for labor market reasons but because of actual or anticipated persecution on the basis of their political ideology, class origin, race, religion, or merely having joined the "wrong" side in a civil war or revolution. Refugees, as with tied movers, would also demonstrate a lesser intensity in the selective characteristics expected of economic migrants. Refugees, for example, include many older adults rather than being primarily young adults. They include workers with skills acquired in school or on the job that are not readily transferable internationally—lawyers, politician, and generals—as well as those with more highly transferable skills—physician, scientists.

Motives for migrating are complex and although it may be tempting to classify international migrants as economic migrants, tied movers, or refugees, more than one factor may be responsible for the migration decision. A person's "economic move" may be encouraged by being reunited with a sibling; a member of a persecuted minority may leave in part because employment opportunities are better elsewhere.

Regardless of the person's motive for migrating, a potential immigrant will seek the visa that is "cheapest" to obtain. A refugee who may not qualify for a refugee visa may seek an occupational preference visa (e.g., some Chilean professionals). Some economic migrants may be able to obtain refugee visas (e.g., some Polish Solidarity members). And, potential economic migrants have married U.S. citizen to obtain a kinship visa.

In practice, the second selection filter, the visa selection process, focuses on those who can satisfy kinship and refugee criteria.

Generally, over 95 percent of immigrants received kinship or refugee visas. In addition, even if a person cannot immigrate under one of the kinship categories, having a relative or friend in the U.S. can be of considerable value in identifying an employer willing and able to help the applicant obtain an occupational preference visa. Thus, the immigration visa rationing system is largely neutral with respect to the skill characteristics of applicants.

The third selective filter which is relevant for unsuccessful visa applicants is whether to become an illegal alien. Illegal immigration may be relatively less costly for immigrants from some countries than others. For a Mexican illegal alien apprehended at the border and who accepts a voluntary departure, the cost of another attempted illegal entry the next night may be small. For a Korean visa abuser (e.g.,violating a student or tourist visa) the cost of another entry includes the difficulty of obtaining a visa as well as the expensive airfare. The greater are the relative costs of illegal immigration from a country, the smaller will be the proportion of unsuccessful visa applicants who will seek to become illegal migrants.[9]

The different incentives for illegal migration have an effect on the relative skill characteristics of those who actually become illegal aliens. There is a nontrivial probability of apprehension and deportation even after having illegally but successfully penetrated the U.S. border. Furthermore, the probability of detection and the costs of deportation are greater if the illegal alien workers are accompanied by dependent family members. This provides an incentive to leave dependents in the country of origin, but it also increases the temporary or cyclical nature of their migration to the U.S. Illegal aliens are more likely than legal immigrants to make investment decisions characteristic of temporary workers. Illegal aliens who make large investments that are specific to the U. S. labor market—whether these investments are occupational, geo-graphic, or firm-specific suffer a greater loss if they are apprehended and deported or simply voluntarily leave the U.S. than otherwise similar illegal aliens with perfectly internationally transferable skills or with very few skills. In addition, skills specific to the country of origin will have depreciated while in the U.S. An illegal alien who returns to the country of origin voluntarily or involuntarily would be at a disadvantage if his skills had depreciated. Furthermore, there is a tendency for the dollar value of country-specific skills to rise with the level of skill, even if it shrinks as a proportion of total skills. For the migration decision, however, it is the dollar value of country-specific skills that plays the central role, not the share. Thus, among unsuccessful visa applicants, the existence of country-specific skills reduces incentives for illegal migration, resulting in the incentives being greatest for those with few if any skills.

Documentation, credentials or licenses are much more likely to be required for jobs that require skill, such as craft or professional occupations, than for many low-skilled jobs. The demonstration of, or application for, the appropriate documentation, credential or license may reveal an illegal alien's presence. That is, an illegal alien is more likely to be detected if he/she applies for a medical, nursing, plumbing or barbering license than if the alien works in a restaurant or nonunion factory job. This documentation effect also implies that incentives for illegal immigration are greater for workers with few skills.

These considerations have implications for the demographic characteristics and skill level of illegal aliens. Illegal aliens are likely to be young adults, either male or female, coming to the U.S. without dependent family members. Although economic migrations tend to be favorably self-selected on the bases of their skill or ability, this is less intense for illegal aliens, and there may even be negative selectivity by skill level. Illegal aliens will tend to have either internationally transferable skills or have few if any skills. The skills of illegal aliens will be lower than those of legal immigrants from the same country of origin, and the relative gap will be greater the higher the skill level of the legal immigrants. Yet, the illegal immigrants will tend to be high-ability, motivated, ambitious, entrepreneurial individuals when compared with other low-skill workers who choose to remain in the origin (Cross and

Sandos, 1981). As they live and work in the U.S., as their U.S. roots deepen, and as they become more permanently attached to the U.S. labor market, the illegal aliens acquire skills specific to their employer, their industry and the U.S. as a whole. As these skills improve, job changes take place and their earnings and employment opportunities expand.

NOTES

[1] A similar picture emerges for the nearly 300 non-Mexican illegal aliens who responded to these questions. Twelve percent did not have running water and 10 percent did not have electricity in their country of origin, but all had both in the U.S. Of those who had a TV or radio in their home country, most (92 percent) had one or more in the U.S. Of those who did not have a TV or radio in their country of origin, 70 percent had one or more in the U.S.

[2] The cost of interior enforcement has been increased by court decisions limiting INS freedom of action in employer "raids" and other activities.

[3] For example, suppose one estimate of the population without illegal aliens is 222 million plus or minus one million, and the other independent estimate which includes illegal aliens is 225 million, also plus or minus one million. The mean difference is 3 million, but the lower and upper bounds are 1 to 5 million. Although the separate estimates of the population have relatively little error (less than one-half of 1 percent in either direction), the difference is subject to a relatively large error (67 percent in either direction).

[4] This is a longer duration of residence than is reported for apprehended illegal aliens, even those who have been in the U.S. for at least one month during their most recent entry. In part, the greater length of stay in the census estimate may reflect the period since they first came to the U.S. to stay (the Census question) rather than the period of time they have been in an illegal status during their most recent stay (the INS question).

Deportable aliens located in 1984 by length of time illegally in the U.S. (excluding certain crewmen):

Percent

Duration	All	In U.S. at least one month
At Entry	54.8	—
Within 72 Hours	22.1	—
4-30 Days	6.6	—
1-6 Months	7.8	47.1
7 Months to 1 Year	2.6	15.6
Over 1 Year	6.2	37.3
Total	100.0	100.0

SOURCE: *1984 Statistical Yearbook of the Immigration and Naturalization Service* (1986) Table ENF 1.4, p. 194.

[5] Within the country limit, colonies and dependencies had a ceiling of 600 visas, which was raised to 5,000 visas in the 1986 Immigration Act.

[6] Enforcement of immigration law in the agricultural sector was made more difficult under the 1986 Act by requiring for the first time search warrants for INS activities on the open areas of farms.

[7] It is easy to show that those with higher levels of ability generally have a greater incentive than those of lesser ability to migrate from a low to a higher income area.

Let W_{ij} be earnings, where $i=0$ in the origin, $i=d$ in the destination, $j=h$ for high-ability workers, and $j=u$ for low-ability workers. The equation $C_j=pW_{oj}+D$ represents the total cost of migration, where p is the proportion of the year devoted to migration and D is the out-of-pocket cost (e.g., airline or bus tickets, cost of moving or acquiring household goods, etc.).

Suppose high-ability workers earn 100k percent more than low-ability workers in both the origin and the destination. Then using the simple formula for the rate of return on an investment that assumes costs occur in the initial period and there is a very long life,

$$r_u = \frac{W_{du} - W_{ou}}{pW_{ou} + D}$$

is the rate of return from migration for the low-ability person. For the high-ability person,

$$r_h = \frac{W_{dh} - W_{oh}}{pW_{oh} + D} = \frac{(1 + k)(W_{du} - W_{ou})}{(1 + k)pW_{ou} + D} = \frac{W_{du} - W_{ou}}{pW_{ou} + D/(1 + k)}.$$

Under the conditions specified, $r_h > r_u$ as long as $D > 0$. The difference between r_h and r_u is smaller the lower is D relative to W_{ou} and p. This argument is strengthened if those with greater labor market ability are also more efficient in migration, that is, they have a lower p or D.

Thus in this simple model those in the origin with greater ability have a greater economic incentive to migrate. The degree of favorable selectivity is smaller if the cost of migrating between the two countries is smaller.

[8] For an analysis of the implications of the distinction between "allocative efficiency" (decisionmaking) and "worker efficiency" (following directions) see T. W. Schultz (1975).

[9] Conceptually, the number of "unsuccessful visa applicants" should include all persons who would apply if a visa were readily available but who do not apply because of the low probability of qualifying under current regulations. These discouraged applicants can be expected to be far more numerous than those who apply and are denied a visa. They are an important source of illegal immigrants.

3
The Survey

In recent years there has been a great public policy interest in illegal aliens. In nearly every session of Congress for the past decade one House or the other has considered legislation, and in 1986 the Immigration Reform and Control Act granted amnesty for certain illegal aliens and imposed sanctions on employers of illegal aliens. Although there have been several commissions and task forces, the advancement in knowledge about illegal aliens and their labor market activities has been remarkably small.[1]

What is perhaps most unique about the public policy debate regarding illegal aliens is the relative absence of systematic social science research. It has not been possible to estimate with precision the size of the illegal alien population or to measure the characteristics of this population. The reason is that illegal aliens have an obvious incentive to avoid contact with survey or census interviewers and, if interviewed, to avoid revealing their status. In the absence of a data base, competing hypotheses regarding the size, characteristics and impact of the illegal alien population can persist. Their persistence may be responsible for the difficulty in developing a consensus in the public policy debate and in Congress, and for the widespread dissatisfaction with the provisions that finally did get enacted.

This chapter reports on the survey methodology developed and implemented for the study of the illegal alien labor market. The survey is the basis for most of the analysis in the substantive chapters that follow. It is a methodology that can have general applicability for the study of the illegal alien labor market, and can be used for the study of other issues. Section I discusses why illegal aliens and their employers are so difficult to study. Section II discusses the methodology used to survey a random sample of apprehended illegal aliens and their employers. The success of the methodology is analyzed in Section III. Section IV is a summary and conclusion.

I. Survey Research on Illegal Aliens

The large increase in public concern with illegal immigration in the past decade can be related to the perception that the number of illegal aliens has increased manyfold. It is, however, not merely the number of illegal aliens that is relevant for understanding their impact on the U.S. The economic and social impact of illegal aliens depends in part on the alien's characteristics. For example, consider two polar examples. The impact of an unskilled illegal alien population locked into dead-end jobs, who move freely and frequently between the U.S. and their home country, would be very different from that of a skilled, upwardly mobile illegal alien population that is permanently settled in this country.

There are many unanswered questions regarding illegal aliens. Are illegal aliens in jobs that are so undesirable that native workers would not take them and hence there is no direct competition in the labor market between illegal aliens and individuals with legal rights to employment? At another extreme, is there such direct competition in the labor market between illegal and legal workers that illegal aliens depress wage and employment opportunities for legal workers with comparable skills? Are illegal aliens in low-wage, dead-end, nonunion jobs with little opportunity for on-the-job training or, given their initial skill level, are they in jobs that provide high wages and training opportunities? Are the employers of illegal aliens small, nonunionized, ethnic enclave employers? Out of a fear of deportation, are illegal aliens held by their employers in a virtual bondage that is little different from slavery? Or do illegal aliens experience considerable voluntary job mobility, working for employers little different from employers in the same region and industry that do not hire illegal workers?

These questions about the employment of illegal aliens cannot be answered merely by analytical reasoning. They are essentially empirical issues. One approach would be to do a survey of employers and to ask them about their employment of illegal aliens, as well as the characteristics of the workplace. This approach, however, would suffer from two major problems. One is that employers might not cooperate in a survey that asked direct questions about illegal alien employment. Until the 1986 Immigration Reform and Control Act which took effect in 1987, it was not against federal law to knowingly employ an illegal alien, and in the few states in which employer sanctions were on the books, the law was not enforced. Yet, many employers, including those who employ illegal aliens, may have been under the false impression that it was illegal (Chiswick and Fullam, 1980). Even if they knew it was not illegal, employers who consider it a "socially undesirable" practice, or who believe others hold this view, might be reluctant to respond truthfully. Similarly, employers skeptical of promises of confidentiality might have been reluctant to respond truthfully out of fear of an Immigration and Naturalization Service (INS) raid.

The second problem with direct inquiries is that employers may not know the legal status of individual workers. When there was no legal requirement to identify an applicant's legal right to work in this country, employers would not wish to incur the expenses of obtaining this knowledge, particularly since direct responses by job applicants may be false. As a result of the new legislation, employers now have to be shown documents (e.g., a passport, birth certificate, or driver's license), but they are not required to ascertain the authenticity of these documents. Perhaps most important, employer perceptions of the legal status of their workers may be quite different from the reality.

A direct survey of illegal aliens themselves would be equally trouble-prone. There is no unbiased sampling frame for illegal aliens. Illegal aliens have an incentive to be nonrespondents in a survey or census for fear of inadvertently revealing their status. Without administrative record checks, even indirect questions on legal status are not likely to generate accurate responses. Some studies use "community contacts" to identify, gain cooperation from and interview illegal aliens. There are numerous biases inherent in this type of haphazard sampling. Different types of illegal aliens may be identified depending on the type of contact. For example, women may predominate if the contact is churches; intact working families with a long stable residence in the U.S. may predominate if the contact is a community group that helps aliens obtain an "adjustment of status"; young males may predominate if the contact is through street corners, bars or pool halls.

Moreover, the types of research questions relevant for a study of illegal aliens and the labor market require microdata on both the illegal alien and the alien's employer. Most workers, regardless of their legal status, would not be able to provide information about many employer and workplace characteristics that are relevant for analytical purposes. The workers would generally not be aware of the type of business organization, the size of the establishment, and the number, schooling, job training and demographic characteristic of the establishment's workforce, among other characteristics. This is more likely to be the situation for relatively new non-English speaking workers who have little familiarity with the U.S. labor market.

II. The Survey Methodology

This section discusses the survey methodology and some of the limitations of the application of the methodology.[2]

(a) Procedures

Whenever an illegal alien is apprehended by the Immigration and Naturalization Service (INS), a form is completed called a Record of Deportable Alien, better known by its form number I-213 (see Exhibit 1). The I-213 is an administrative record kept in the local INS office, although summary statistics are transmitted to INS headquarters in Washington, D.C. for management purposes and publication in the INS *Annual Report* and *Statistical Yearbook.*

The I-213 includes information on the name and address of the alien, as well as on the alien's demographic characteristics (such as date of birth, sex, marital status, number of children). It also includes questions on immigration characteristics, such as when and where the alien last entered the U.S., immigrant status at entry, method of location of the alien, country of last permanent residence, and nationality, as well as the nationality of the alien's spouse, parents and children. The labor market information includes the name and address of the current or most recent employer in the U.S., the period of employment, and the wage rate. The I-213 forms filed in the interior, as distinct from the border area, are nearly always completed in full, although the degree of truthfulness of the responses is open to question. The information on the I-213 regarding the current or most recent employer permits these forms to be used as a sampling frame for a survey of the employers of apprehended illegal aliens.

Results from a survey of employers of illegal aliens cannot be interpreted in isolation. The distinguishing characteristics of their employers can be determined only by knowing how employers that either do not employ illegal aliens or who are randomly selected from the population of employers respond to the same questions. It is not possible to develop a sample of employers who do not employ illegal aliens. Indeed, even an employer cannot be certain that there are no illegal aliens in the workforce. On the other hand, randomly selected employers from lists of establishments can be used as a benchmark if it is assumed that not all employers hire illegal aliens, or that the proportion of illegal aliens in the workforce is larger among those establishments identified by an illegal alien.

Thus, the survey methodology adopted for this project was to draw a stratified random sample of I-213 forms filed in an INS District Office (interior) and to transcribe on an "abstract form" the relevant demographic, immigrant and labor market data, including the identity of the alien's employer. The employers identified in this manner are referred to as the "INS sample." A "general sample" of employers is identified by drawing a random sample from standard lists or directories of establishments in the same geographic area.

The methodology was implemented for the Chicago SMSA using the I-213 forms filed in the Chicago District Office of INS during 1983. A pilot study (Chiswick and Fullam, 1980) indicated that greater statistical efficiency could be achieved for the same budget by using stratified sampling for the I-213 forms. Three industry categories (manufacturing, restaurant and other services) and two country-of-origin categories (Mexican and non-Mexican) resulted in six cells. The stratification was done because of the greater homogeneity of some of the key study variables in the restaurant sector and the overwhelming number of I-213 forms for Mexican nationals in the INS Chicago files. For each month in 1983, the I-213 forms for male illegal aliens with an "identifiable" employer were separated into the six strata and systematic sampling was employed.[3] For employers identified by more than one sampled alien, random sampling was used to select only one identifying alien.

The general sample of employers was developed by systematic random sampling of directories within each of the three industries. The sources for establishments in the Chicago SMSA were the Illinois Manufacturers Directory (1984), the Illinois Services Directory (1984), and restaurant listings in the 1984 Yellow Pages telephone directories for the Chicago SMSA.

A double-blind interviewing procedure was used so that the interviewers and respondents would not be influenced by knowing the specific source for the name and address of the establishment. The interviewers were told that the purpose of the study was to learn about the hiring needs and practices of employers in different types of industries, and that the employers had been randomly selected from various directories and listings for the Chicago metropolitan area. The specific directories and listings were not mentioned and at no time were the interviewers informed that a portion of the sample had been taken from INS records. The establishments were provided the same information as the interviewers regarding the nature of the study and the source of the sample cases.

The questionnaire was designed to obtain a wide range of data regarding the characteristics of the establishment and the workforce (see Exhibit 2). The survey instrument began with general questions regarding ownership, number of employees, their racial and ethnic composition, schooling level, provision of on-the-job training, unionization and wage rates, among other variables. A set of questions on new hires, number employed, and reasons for terminations were then asked regarding several demographic groups —young workers, older workers, adult males, adult females and "recent immigrants." Recent immigrants were defined as individuals in the U.S. less than five years. There were no direct questions about the hiring or employment of illegal aliens.

The interviews were to be conducted with the person at the establishment who was in charge of hiring for the most typical male nonsupervisory job. The interviewers were instructed to seek a face-to-face interview.[4] If the respondent seemed hesitant, the interviewer was to offer the respondent a summary of the survey findings.[5] A second procedure to avoid a refusal was to offer to conduct the interview by telephone if the interviewer thought that a telephone interview was feasible. Last, a monetary incentive of $15 for the establishment could be offered as a token compensation for the respondent's time. Interviewers were instructed to offer the stipend only after having exhausted all other alternatives for gaining cooperation and only when the respondent indicated he or she was "too busy to spare the time," "could not waste company time" or gave similar reasons for refusing to be interviewed. To discourage interviewers from offering the stipend too readily and because of the potentially high cost of such an open-ended offer, the interviewers knew in advance that each had a maximum limit of six stipends that could be given.

(b) Limitations

One limitation of the sampling methodology is that INS apprehensions at the Chicago District Office are not likely to constitute a random sample of the resident illegal alien population in the Chicago metropolitan area. Illegal aliens who have less experience or who are less adept at avoiding detection are more likely to be apprehended. In addition, at various times the INS has targeted its limited enforcement resources on particular segments of the illegal alien population.

There was apparently no particular targeting emphasis in effect at the Chicago District Office during 1983. Furthermore, the aliens were brought to the INS's attention through a variety of mechanisms, including INS-initiated establishment raids, "referrals" from the police arising mainly from traffic violations, brawls and petty crime, "snitching" by former lovers, jealous co-workers and angry neighbors, as well as "walk-ins," those who turn themselves in to the INS because they believe they could qualify for legal status. The greater the variety in methods of location of illegal aliens, the more closely the apprehensions may approximate a random sample of the resident illegal alien population.

Another limitation of the methodology is the different nature of the probability of inclusion in the two employer samples. Employers of illegal aliens are more likely to be in the INS sample the greater the proportion of illegal aliens among their workers and the larger the number of workers. The probability of inclusion in the general sample is largely independent of the number of workers. While this difference affects the average size of the establishments in the two samples, it should not affect other comparisons when establishment size is held constant.

III. Evaluation of the Survey Methodology

The survey methodology is evaluated in this section to determine the effectiveness of the procedures, and to offer insights that would be useful for future employer surveys, particularly on potentially sensitive topics.

(a) Eligible Establishments

The INS Record of Deportable Alien (I-213) was used to identify establishments known to have employed an apprehended illegal alien. The probability that an establishment is in this sample is directly related to the proportion of illegal aliens in its workforce and the number of employees. Both factors are relevant if the probability of an illegal alien being apprehended is purely random, but they are even more important if INS targets its enforcement activities towards establishments believed to be employing a larger number of illegal aliens.

The general samples of employers were randomly selected from industry-based directories of establishments. For these establishments, the probability of being sampled is independent of the number of employees, except to the extent that size may influence inclusion in the directory listing.

Thus, the two sampling frames offer different probabilities of selection as a function of the establishment's size. This influenced the proportion of sample cases classified as ineligible because they had five or fewer employees. In the INS sample, 19 establishments out of the 292 sample cases (6.5 percent) were identified as having five or fewer employees, in contrast with the 67 establishments out of 371 sample cases (18.1 percent) in the general sample. This same phenomenon undoubtedly influenced the finding that the average number of employees in the INS sample exceeds that in the general sample.

The general sample also included a larger proportion of cases where, in spite of a name and address, it was not possible to locate the establishment. This may have arisen because of the greater proportion of smaller firms, some of which may have closed or moved without leaving an easily obtained forwarding address. In addition, the "current" directory listings were older than the INS arrest records, and may therefore have contained more errors.

(b) Locating the INS Sample of Establishments in Directories

The INS sample included only employers for whom sufficient information was provided by the alien so that the employer might reasonably be located. Through telephone listings and interviewer visits to the address, it was possible to locate nearly all of the employers. Yet, for various reasons, relying on telephone listings alone would have proved inadequate. It was not possible to locate in telephone directories a surprising 31.2 percent of the establishments. Nearly all of the restaurants were identified in phone directories (only 1 percent were not identified), but 29 percent of the manufacturing establishments and a surprising 61 percent of the "other service" establishments could not be located in telephone directories. Within industry categories, there was no significant difference between establishments identified by a Mexican or a non-Mexican illegal alien in the proportion located in phone directories.

In some instances the respondent may have provided a different company name than is used in the phone listing. In service industries, such as lawn care, the establishment's "location" may be ambiguous and hence the greater difficulty in locating the establishment.

These findings suggest potential difficulties in using phone directories as a sampling frame for employer surveys in manufacturing and especially in service industries other than restaurants. They also suggest the difficulty of trying to computer-match establishments identified from two separate sources based on surveys or administrative records. Supplementing telephone listings with interviewer visits was responsible for the final high match rate.

(c) Interview Completion Rates

Among the 497 establishments deemed eligible for an interview and for whom interview attempts were made, 76 were classified as refusals and 421 were actually interviewed. This is an interview rate of 84.7 percent overall, 84.0 percent in the INS sample and 85.4 percent in the general (directory) sample. No interviews were terminated before the final questions.

Of the 421 interviews, 15 were classified as "partial interviews" because of the large amount of missing data.[6] Excluding partial interviews, the "completion rate," defined as complete interviews (406) divided by total interviews and refusals (497), was 81.7 percent (table 3-1). The rate is 79.4 percent in the INS sample and 83.9 percent in the general sample.

The completion rate may also be defined very conservatively as the number of completed (nonpartial) interviews (406) divided by the total number of cases not deemed to be ineligible (524). For a variety of reasons, a disposition of interviewed, ineligible or refused could not be given at the close of the field period for 27 establishments. Some of these establishments had been contacted but requested a scheduling of the interview beyond the field period, others requested to be called back, and for some others the appropriate respondent had not yet been identified. Calculating the conservative completion rate, 77.5 percent of the establishments were completed interviews, 76.0 percent in the INS sample and 78.9 percent in the general sample.[7]

Although it had been expected that employers of illegal aliens would be much more hesitant about participating in a survey of hiring practices than randomly selected employers, the very small

Table 3-1

Final Disposition of Sample of Establishments

Sample source & stratum	Fielded sample	Ineligible[a]	Eligible Number (percent)[d]	Completed interviews[b] Number (percent)[d]	Refusals Number (percent)[d]	Other eligible non-interviews[c] Number (percent)[d]
INS sample						
1 Mex.-Manuf.	69	5	64 (100)	46 (72)	11 (17)	7 (11)
2 Mex.-Rest.	58	8	50 (100)	35 (70)	14 (28)	1 (2)
3 Mex.-Serv.	60	6	54 (100)	40 (74)	7 (13)	7 (13)
4 Non-Mex.-Manuf.	45	4	41 (100)	35 (85)	4 (10)	2 (5)
5 Non-Mex.-Rest.	26	4	22 (100)	15 (68)	2 (9)	5 (23)
6 Non-Mex.-Serv.	34	11	23 (100)	22 (96)	1 (4)	0 (0)
Subtotal	292	38	254 (100)	193 (76)	39 (15)	22 (9)
General sample						
7 Manuf.	138	26	112 (100)	90 (80)	19 (17)	3 (3)
8 Rest.	100	44	56 (100)	39 (70)	6 (11)	11 (19)
9 Serv.	133	31	102 (100)	84 (82)	12 (12)	6 (6)
Subtotal	371	101	270 (100)	213 (79)	37 (14)	20 (7)
Total	663	139	524 (100)	406 (77)	76 (15)	42 (8)

a. Ineligible includes firms with fewer than 5 workers, establishments gone out of business and duplicate cases.

b. Excludes 15 partial interviews.

c. Includes 15 partial interviews and establishments not interviewed at the close of the field period.

d. Percent of eligible cases.

(and statistically insignificant) difference in each of the measures of completion and interview rates suggests that this was not the case.

(d) The Incentive Stipend

The "incentive stipend" was one method used by the interviewers to encourage respondent cooperation. Interviewers were instructed to offer the establishment a $15 stipend for the time of the respondent as a last ditch effort to prevent a refusal.[8] The open-ended nature of the potential financial obligation was a considerable concern. In addition to emphasizing to the interviewers that the incentive was to be used only as a last resort, each of the interviewers had a survey maximum of only six stipends that could be granted to employers.

Of the 601 applicable situations, the stipend was offered in only 32 instances. The interviewers were far more cautious than had been expected. With this caution, it is reasonable to assume that there would otherwise have been no interviews with these 32 establishments. Interestingly, 17 of the 32 establishments (53 percent) offered the incentive consented to be interviewed and completed the questionnaire. Most surprising, however, was the fact that 14 of the 17 who consented *declined* to accept the funds. The stipend was actually granted in only three instances.

The stipend was accepted by two small manufacturing establishments (average size 16 employees) and one large service establishment (197 employees). On average, there was no difference in firm size between the three establishments that accepted the stipend and the 14 influenced by the incentive but who did not accept it. There was also no pattern between acceptance of the stipend and whether the establishment was privately owned or part of a (nonfamily) corporation. There was, however, an effect of whether the respondent was an owner (sole owner or partner) or an employee. Of the 4 owner-respondents, 2 accepted the stipend, whereas of the 13 employee-respondents only 1 accepted the stipend.

The interviewers reported that the offer of a stipend seemed to convey to the respondents a greater sense of seriousness or professionalism regarding the survey, thereby eliciting a more favorable response. The magnitude of the stipend was presumably sufficiently small that the actual receipt of the funds was generally not a consideration. The combination of offering a modest financial incentive as a last-ditch effort to prevent a refusal and the limit on the number of stipends each interviewer could grant appear to have been a successful low-cost technique for discouraging refusals.

(e) Reworking Refusals

The procedures developed for reworking initial refusals also appear to have been successful. Of the 126 initial refusals, it was concluded that 24 were not likely to be converted, primarily because the respondent indicated that participating in the survey was against company policy or the company's attorney advised against participating (table 3-2). Based on their characteristics, the other establishments were assigned to be reworked either by another one of the project's face-to-face interviewers, by a professional telephone interviewer, or by the Chicago coordinating staff.

Overall, 45 of the 102 establishments assigned for reworking consented to an interview. This resulted in a refusal conversion rate of 36 percent (45 out of 126). As there were four partial interviews, the refusal conversion rate for complete interviews was 33 percent (41 out of 126).

Although the sample size is small, the ratio of partial interviews to all interviews was higher in the refusal conversion than in the full sample, 8.9 percent as compared to 3.6 percent. This is not surprising since these establishments were initially less inclined to grant an interview.

It is not possible to evaluate the separate effectiveness of the three procedures for reworking refusals since the assignments were not random. For example, although the Chicago coordinating staff had the lowest conversion rate, they were also assigned the establishments that were viewed as the most difficult to interview. Overall, however, the refusal conversion procedures appear to have been successful and worth the additional effort.

Table 3-2

**Final Disposition of Initial Refusals
by Whether Reworked and by Method of Interview**

	Total	Interview[a]	Refusal	Ineligible
Assigned to be reworked	102	45	52	5
Face-to-face interviewers	17	9	8	—
Telephone interviewers (b)	74	33	36	5
Coordinating staff (by telephone) (c)	11	3	8	—
Not assigned for reworking	24			
Total Initial Refusals	126			

a. Includes 4 interviews later dispositioned as partials; 3 of these were completed by the telephone interviewers and 1 was completed face-to-face.

b. Professional telephone interviewers trained for reworking the refusals for this survey.

c. Project coordinator and Field coordinator for the survey.

(f) Item Nonresponse

Item nonresponse can be a serious limitation on the usefulness of survey data. Beyond some point, extensive item nonresponse is functionally equivalent to refusing to participate. Although some surveys and censuses impute values for nonresponse, this was not done for this survey.

Item nonresponse may arise for two fundamental reasons. One is that the respondent, in truth, does not know the answer or has only such vague information that the respondent does not wish to offer a specific response. These are the truthful "don't know" responses. The other is that the respondent knows the answer but refuses to reveal the data. It is difficult to disentangle reasons for item nonresponse. Although both types of item nonresponse are evident in this survey, in general the response rate to individual questions was very high.

(i) *Partial Interviews*—On the basis of item nonresponse, 15 of the 421 interviews were classified as partial interviews and 406 were classified as completed interviews. This classification was done without regard for the sample from which the employer was selected and was based on predetermined criteria. An interview was classified "partial" if at least 20 percent of the responses were "don't know," blanks or invalid codes. Since no interviews were terminated before the end of the questionnaire, this was not a source of partial interviews.

The 15 partial interviews included 11 from the illegal alien (INS) sample and 4 from the general sample of employers.[9] The proportion of partial interviews, that is, partial interviews as a percent of all interviews, was 5.4 percent for the INS sample, 6.9 percent for the Mexican aliens and 2.7 percent for the non-Mexican aliens. The rate was 1.8 percent for the general sample. Although these differences are small, they suggest somewhat greater difficulty in eliciting responses from the employers of Mexican illegal aliens, even though neither they nor the interviewers knew the source for the identification of the employers or the survey interest in illegal aliens. Partial interviews were nearly equally frequent in manufacturing and other services, but did not arise in the restaurant sector.

The analysis of item nonresponse suggests that partial interviews were more frequent in larger establishments with lower-skilled workers in jobs with high labor turnover. If so, many if not most of the "don't knows" in the partial interviews may have been truthful responses.

(ii) *Completed Interviews*—Among the 406 interviews classified as complete, the item nonresponse rates were very low for nearly all questions.

The establishments had the greatest difficulty responding to the question on the educational distribution of those currently employed (table 3-3). The nonresponse rate for the educational distribution of current employees was 12.3 percent overall, 16.6 percent for the INS sample of employers and 8.5 percent for the

Table 3-3
Item Nonresponse Rates for Completed Interviews
for Questions with High Nonresponse rates[a]
(percent)

Questions	INS sample	General sample	All
Nonimmigrant questions:			
Educational attainment of workers	16.6	8.5	12.3
Wages by educational level	5.2	4.7	4.9
Length of training if no previous experience	8.3	11.7	10.1
Length of training if experienced in job	5.7	4.2	4.9
Reason adult men left establishment	5.9	3.5	4.9
Reason adult women left establishment	4.9	2.2	3.7
Immigrant-related questions:			
Recent immigrants hired in past year	1.9	0.0	1.3
Current employment of recent immigrants	8.3	4.2	6.2
Reason immigrant men left establishment	1.1	8.0	2.6
Reason immigrant women left establishment	6.1	11.1	7.1

a. Calculated as nonresponse to question (including "don't know," blanks and refusals) as percentage of combined total of valid responses and nonresponses. Totals vary from question to question because not all questions were asked of all respondents.

general sample. It is not obvious that this reflects a reluctance to answer the question. It is to be expected that employers, particularly those with a large immigrant component of the workforce, would be less knowledgeable about the level of formal schooling of their workers than many other characteristics. Both sets of employers had some difficulty, although less so, responding to the question on wages paid by educational level. The nonresponse rate for this set of questions was about 5 percent in each sample.

The number of days of training required for a newly hired worker to learn to do well the most common male nonsupervisory job also generated some difficulty, particularly if the worker did not have prior experience. The nonresponse rate was 5 percent if the worker was experienced in the job and 10 percent if the worker had no previous experience (table 3-3). This may reflect the greater difficulty in specifying the number of days of training required for workers with greater variation in prior work experience. The reasons why adult men and women left the establishment also had high item nonresponse rates, but these too may reflect truthful answers.

Perhaps the most important difference in item nonresponse rates between the sample of illegal alien employers and the general sample is the greater proportion of the former who did not respond to the question on the current employment of recent immigrants (i.e., immigrants in the U.S. less than five years). The rates were 8 percent and 4 percent, respectively (table 3-3). Item nonresponse rates were lower for the question on the number of recent immigrants hired in the past year. The high nonresponse rates in the general sample for why male and female recent immigrants left the establishment in the past year are not statistically reliable because of the very small number of establishments that reported the departure of any recent immigrant workers. Part of the difficulty employers had with the "recent immigrant" questions may be a consequence of their not knowing how long their foreign-born workers have been in the U.S. This difficulty may be greater for the stock of workers than for the flow (new hires).

The questionnaire often required that the sum of the numerical responses to a set of questions equal a previously given total (e.g., that the racial/ethnic and sex distribution of employees sum to the total). Establishments were given the option of reporting components as absolute numbers or as percents. The interviewers had hand calculators with them in order to check that the sum equaled the previously given total, and sought a reconciliation from the respondent if this was not the case. In spite of some initial misgivings about adding this complexity to the questionnaire, the interviewers reported that the procedure went smoothly. The requirement that these items sum to their previously reported total did not increase the nonresponse rate or apparently place an undue burden on the interviewer or respondent. Reconciliation on the spot proved to be much more effective than reconciliation after leaving the interview, and reduced the number of invalid (i.e., inconsistent) responses.

(iii) *Summary*—The analysis indicates that nonresponse rates were generally very low. Nonresponse rates were higher for questions that required information on the educational attainment of employees and on the reasons why employees left the establishment. There is some evidence that employers initially reluctant to participate in the survey were more likely to grant interviews with higher nonresponse rates, and hence were also more likely to be classified as partial interviews. Partial interviews appeared only in the service and manufacturing sectors, and were more common among the establishments identified by an apprehended Mexican illegal alien. Among completed interviews, there is some evidence of higher nonresponse rates for the employers of illegal aliens, but the difference is very small. Overall, item nonresponse does not appear to have been a problem in this survey.

(g) Length of Interview

The length of a completed interview is calculated as the difference between the time of the start and finish of the interview, including interruptions when there was no lengthy break in contact. The length can be computed for 395 of the 406 completed interviews. It is not computed for the one (authorized) self-administered interview for an establishment of over 2,700 employees, when the ending time was not recorded, or when there was a lengthy break in contact, including a continuation of the interview on the following workday.

The range of interview length was from 10 minutes for two small establishments (13 and 50 employees) to 151 minutes (a service sector establishment with 30 employees). The average length was

35.5 minutes, with little difference among industries, but with the interview taking about 6 minutes longer in establishments in the INS sample (table 3-4). Other things the same, interview length rises

Table 3-4

Mean and Standard Deviation of Length of Interview in Minutes, by Industry and Sample[a]

Industry	INS sample	General sample	Total
Manufacturing	39.75	31.95	35.35
	(18.08)	(13.04)	(15.87)
Restaurant	34.80	33.28	34.18
	(10.13)	(12.51)	(11.34)
Service	41.10	32.99	36.65
	(24.37)	(19.64)	(22.19)
Total	38.72	32.57	35.51
	(18.70)	(15.59)	(17.40)

NOTE: Number of observations=395.
a. Standard deviations in parentheses.

significantly with the number of employees (SIZE), is 3 minutes longer if the employer had been identified by an illegal alien (ILLEMP), and is 6 minutes longer if the interview was done in person (FACE) rather than over the phone.[10] It should be noted, however, that phone interviews (28 percent of the interviews) were generally limited to situations in which it was expected there would be fewer interruptions, rather than allocated solely through random assignment. There were no significant differences by industry (REST, SERVICE, with manufacturing as the benchmark) when other variables were held constant.

IV. Summary and Conclusions

This chapter discussed the methodology of the 1984 Chicago metropolitan area survey of the employers of illegal aliens. These employers were identified by an apprehended illegal alien on the

INS Record of Deportable Alien (I-213) completed in the INS Chicago District Office in 1983. Demographic, labor market and migration data on the illegal alien were transcribed from the I-213 form. A parallel sample of establishments was selected from standard directories. Stratified random sampling was used.

The resulting data file is unique for research on illegal aliens. It includes matched employee-employer data—data on the employee (illegal alien) from the I-213 and on the employer from the establishment survey. It also includes establishment data obtained in an identical manner from employers randomly selected from standard directories.

An attempt to locate establishments identified on the INS I-213 forms and in standard directories solely by telephone listing demonstrated the difficulty of matching establishments identified in separate administrative records. Supplementing telephone listings with interviewer visits was responsible for the very high final match rate.

The survey methodology for interviewing establishments about their characteristics and their workforce appears to have been successful. There was no difficulty in obtaining the target of at least 400 completed interviews from the 663 establishments selected in the sampling procedures. There were 406 completed interviews, excluding 15 interviews classified as partial interviews because of missing information.

Offering a small ($15) stipend to the establishment if it seemed that a refusal to participate was likely appears to have been a successful low-cost procedure. The quota on the number of stipends each interviewer could grant encouraged the interviewers to use it selectively. The offer seems to have conveyed a greater sense of seriousness and professionalism. Overall, 14 of the 17 establishments that consented to the interview only after the offer of the stipend declined the funds. Acceptance of the funds was more likely if the respondent was also the owner.

The probability that an establishment would be in the INS sample is a positive function of the number of employees, but this is not the case for the general sample. As a result, the number of ineligible establishments (fewer than five employees) is greater in the general sample, and the average number of employees in the eligible establishments is larger in the INS sample.

The conservative completion rate, that is, completed interviews as a percent of all cases not known to be ineligible, was 77 percent overall. It was 76 percent in the INS sample and 79 percent in the general sample. Thus, the samples did not differ in the interview completion rate.

Although partial interviews and item nonresponse were more common in the INS sample, the differences were very small. Item nonresponse rates were generally very low, although establishments had some difficulty with certain questions. These included reporting the level of schooling of their current workers, wages by schooling level, reasons why employees left the establishments, and current employment of persons who were "recent" immigrants. It is not surprising that these are the data elements with which the employers had the most difficulty. The nonresponses appear to be genuine "don't knows" rather than attempts to conceal information.

The survey procedures developed for this project appear to have been very successful for generating a unique data file on the illegal alien labor market. The survey methodology could be applied elsewhere for the study of illegal aliens. In addition, many features of the methodology could be used fruitfully for other surveys of employers, particularly on other sensitive issues.

NOTES

[1] For example, consider the activities of the Congressionally appointed Select Commission on Immigration and Refugee Policy, whose primary mandate was to study and make recommendations regarding illegal aliens. The commission funded virtually no research on illegal aliens in the United States, and in its research report reprinted results of illegal alien research completed long before

the commission was established. As a result, a major study effort failed to advance knowledge in this area. See, Select Commission (1981).

2 For a detailed discussion of the survey methodology, see Chiswick (1985, Volume I, chapter 2). The questionnaire, interviewer training manual and other documents related to conducting the survey are reproduced in Chiswick (1985, Volume II).

3 The survey was limited to men primarily because of the small number of illegal alien women apprehended by the Chicago District Office.

4 Preference was to be given to face-to-face interviewing, although in certain circumstances telephone interviews were conducted. Initial contacts were by a letter from the Principal Investigator, followed by either a telephone or in-person contact by the interviewer. Since most of the initial contact of the establishment by the interviewers was to be by telephone, the face-to-face interviewers were chosen for their skills in face-to-face and telephone interviewing.

5 Offering a summary of findings written in nontechnical terms that would be relevant for the respondent's industry generated considerable interest. Of the 421 employers interviewed, 155 requested a summary of findings. The specially prepared summary included cross-tabulations of wages, unionization and other variables by industry and size of establishment, without reference to illegal aliens.

6 Using predetermined criteria, interviews were classified as partial if 20 percent or more of the responses were "don't know," blanks or invalid codes. Partial interviews are discussed below in greater detail.

7 These completion rates are on a par with the results from the small sample pilot survey of illegal alien employers conducted earlier (Chiswick and Fullam, 1980). In the pilot survey 78 percent of the 39 eligible illegal alien employers completed the interviews.

8 For many small firms this would in effect be a direct payment by check to the respondent/owner.

9 Distribution of partial interviews:

Sample	Manuf.	Restaurant	Other services	Total
INS Sample	7	0	4	11
Mexican Alien	5	0	4	9
Non-Mexican Alien	2(a)	0	0	2
General Sample	1	0	3	4
All	8	0	7	15

(a) One from Europe/Canada, one from Other Latin America.

[10] Regression analysis of length of interview (LENGTH) in minutes:

Variable	Coefficient	t-ratio
SIZE	0.031	3.13
SIZE SQUARED	-0.000008	-1.37
REST	-1.130	-0.51
SERVICE	1.524	0.80
ILLEMP	3.139	1.76
FACE	6.009	3.17
CONSTANT	27.038	14.11
R^2	0.124	
Adjusted R^2	0.111	
Number of observations	395	

4

Illegal Alien Labor Market Behavior

This chapter examines the labor market behavior of the sample of illegal aliens apprehended in the metropolitan Chicago labor market. Particular attention is devoted to the analysis of their wages and the characteristics of their employers. Wages are perhaps the best single measure of adjustment in the labor market. The wage analysis focuses on the effects of duration in the U.S., country of origin, and method of entry, among other variables. The analysis of employer characteristics focuses on the extent to which illegal aliens experience job mobility. The greater their job mobility the more likely are they to receive wages approximating their maximum productivity and the greater their opportunities for upward mobility. While there are no direct data on the issue of the "exploitation" of illegal aliens, a heated political issue, exploitation is minimized when there are opportunities for job mobility.

In this chapter the illegal alien is the unit of observation. Most of the analysis is based on the data abstracted from the INS Record of Deportable Alien (I-213) for nearly 300 apprehended illegal aliens. For a subsample of nearly 200 aliens, the data on the alien's characteristics are matched with the employer survey responses. This provides a rather unique data file, not merely for the analysis of illegal aliens, but also for labor market analysis in general—a data file that combines worker and employer/workplace characteristics. Sample sizes are reduced, however, to the extent there are missing values for one or more of the variables in the analysis. To preserve the integrity of the data there was no imputation of missing values.

Section I describes the characteristics of the sample of illegal aliens using standard descriptive statistics. Section II is the multivariate statistical analysis of wages of the illegal aliens. In section III, the employer characteristics of illegal aliens are analyzed analytically and statistically. This is followed by a discussion of exploitation of illegal aliens in section IV. The chapter closes (section V) with a summary and conclusion.

I. Descriptive Statistics

The data on the illegal alien from the INS administrative record, the I-213, include age, nationality, marital status, method of entry, duration in the U.S. in the most recent stay, and wages (see Exhibit 1). Unfortunately there are no data on the person's schooling and the quality of the reported "occupation" was too poor for these data to be transcribed. The employer data are from the lengthy survey and include a variety of information about the characteristics of the establishment and its workforce (see Exhibit 2). Because of the nature of the study, it was not possible to ask the employer questions about the alien who identified the establishment.

To increase statistical efficiency, subject to the project's budget constraint, stratified sampling was used. The count of illegal aliens by origin and industry does not reflect their proportion in the population of apprehended illegal aliens. In the sample of 292 apprehended illegal aliens, 64 percent were Mexican nationals, 7 percent were from Europe and Canada, 20 percent were from other parts of the Americas, and 9 percent were from the rest of the world (table 4-1).[1] Although data were not available on the illegal alien's total length of stay in U.S., there are data on the duration of the current stay. About 20 percent of the sample had been in the U.S. for less than 6 months, 8 percent for 7 to 12 months, 38 percent for more than 1 but less than 4 years, 26 percent for more than 4 but

Table 4-1

Distribution of Apprehended Illegal
Aliens by Duration in the U.S. and Country of Origin

Duration up to	Mexico	Europe, Canada	Other Latin Amer.	Asia, Africa, other	No data	Total (percent)
6 months	48	1	8	1	0	58 (19.9)
1 year	13	0	6	3	0	22 (7.5)
2 years	21	5	13	8	0	47 (16.1)
3 years	16	5	5	4	0	30 (10.3)
4 years	22	2	5	3	0	32 (11.0)
5 years	17	5	7	3	0	32 (11.0)
6 years	11	0	2	1	1	15 (5.1)
7 years	7	0	2	0	0	9 (3.1)
8 years	14	0	5	0	0	19 (6.5)
9 years	4	1	0	0	0	5 (1.7)
10 years	4	0	2	0	0	6 (2.1)
11 years	3	0	1	0	0	4 (1.4)
12 or more years	7	0	1	2	0	10 (3.4)
No data	0	1	0	2	0	3 (1.0)
Total	187	20	57	27	1	292
Percent	64.0	6.9	19.5	9.3	0.3	100.0

less than 8 years, and 9 percent for 8 or more years. This is considerably longer than the average length of the most recent stay for all illegal aliens apprehended by INS. But a longer length of stay is to be expected for illegal aliens apprehended in the interior of the country.

In the sample, nearly all of the Mexican illegal aliens (96 percent) and most of those from other parts of Latin American (79 percent) were EWIs, that is, they had entered the U.S. without inspection (table 4-2). Most of the European/Canadian

Table 4-2
Status at Entry of Apprehended
Illegal Aliens by Country of Origin

Country	EWI[a]	Visitor	Student	Other	Total
Mexico	179	6	0	2	187
Europe/ Canada	0	18	0	2	20
Other Latin Amer	45	10	0	2	57
Asia/Af-rica/ Other[b]	0	21	5	2	28
Total	224	55	5	8	292

a. EWI is "entry without inspection."
b. Includes one observation with country not reported.

illegal aliens had violated a visitor visa, while most of the illegal aliens from Asia, Africa, the Middle East or elsewhere violated a visitor or student visa. These patterns are very similar to the distribution of method of entry discussed in chapter 2 for all apprehended illegal aliens.

The apprehended male illegal aliens in the Chicago sample had an average age of 30.6 years, had been in the U.S. illegally for an average of only 3.4 years during their most recent stay, and slightly more than half of the sample (55 percent) reported they were not married. Thus, the sample can be characterized as being comprised of young adult, unmarried men who have been in the U.S. a relatively short period of time. This characterization has been found in other studies. The 1975 David North-Marion Houstoun nationwide sample of nearly 800 apprehended illegal aliens also concluded that they were predominantly single young adults. In the North-

Houstoun sample, the average age for the men was 29 years and their average duration for all stays was 3.2 years (Chiswick, 1984).

A survey of Mexican illegal aliens who had returned to their home villages in the state of Jalisco, a major source of illegal migrants, also found that at the time of the illegal migration they were predominantly young adult single males with low levels of education (Diez-Canedo, 1980). However, they did not come from the poorest of families, which cannot afford to finance the migration. They tended to be "underemployed" members of families that owned or had access to farmland, rather than day laborers.

The characterization of illegal aliens as young, single and recent arrivals is not limited to men. A comparative study for Los Angeles of legal and illegal alien women born in Mexico also found that the illegal aliens are young, single and recently arrived compared to legal immigrants (Simon and De Ley, 1984).

The relatively short duration in the U.S. of apprehended illegal aliens, about three years, may be contrasted with the longer average duration of immigrants in census data. In the 1980 Census, among adult foreign-born men the average duration in the U.S. was 18.3 years for white immigrants (excluding Hispanics), 13.0 years for Mexican immigrants, and 9.2 for Asian immigrants.

Part of the difference in duration of residence in the U.S. between legal and illegal aliens may be due to the very rapid increase in illegal immigration in recent years, which lowers the average duration in the U.S. of the stock of illegal aliens. Another explanation may be a greater extent of return migration for illegal aliens, thereby reducing the relative proportion with a long period of residence. For many illegal aliens, particularly from Mexico, the migration is viewed as a mechanism for capital accumulation to buy a house or invest in a business when they return home. Hence, for many, illegal migration is a temporary phenomenon, with newer and younger cohorts replenishing older cohorts.

In addition, with a longer duration of residence, some illegal aliens acquire permanent resident alien status through either regular immigration procedures (e.g., obtaining a visa as a relative of a U.S. citizen or resident alien) or an "adjustment of status" when apprehended. There may also be a difference in measurement concepts with the illegal alien data referring to time actually in the U.S. during their most recent stay and the census data referring to the length of time since the person first came to the U.S.

Finally, the probability that an illegal alien is apprehended can be expected to decline with duration of residence. The knowledge and skills acquired through living and working in the U.S. can be expected to increase the alien's ability to avoid detection. Or, alternatively, those illegal aliens with characteristics associated with a high probability of apprehension are arrested sooner rather than later. If so, the average duration in the U.S. of apprehended illegal aliens would underestimate the average duration of all illegal aliens.

It is the relatively low duration of residence of the apprehended illegal aliens that accounts for their young average age and high proportion who are not married. In general, inter-regional and international migrants tend to be young and unmarried. And these characteristics are more intense for migrants who view the move as temporary, or as part of a circular migration.

An important characteristic of the I-213 data is information on wages. An hourly wage is generally reported. For respondents who reported their wage on some other basis (e.g., day or week) the data were converted to an hourly wage by assuming full-time employment.

The average hourly wage at the time of apprehension in 1983 was $4.52 for the entire sample, with Mexican nationals receiving $4.42 and other nationals receiving $4.73. These rates are substantially in excess of the federal legal minimum wage of $3.35 that was applicable during this period. Very few of the illegal aliens reported a wage below the federal legal minimum; only 45 illegal aliens (16 percent) out of the 279 workers for whom a wage was reported. Of these, 18 were in the restaurant industry (of whom 12 were Mexican nationals), 26 were in other services (16 Mexicans), and 1 (a non-Mexican) was in manufacturing. The federal minimum wage is lower than $3.35 per hour for those in the restaurant sector where a tip-credit may be applicable (e.g., busboys). Also, the procedure for estimating the hourly wage may have resulted in its being underestimated for workers in part-time employment who reported a daily rate or a weekly salary. Yet, the absence of full compliance with federal minimum wage laws cannot be discounted (Ashenfelter and Smith, 1979).

II. Analysis of Wages

The hourly wages of illegal aliens are analyzed in this section using data on the illegal alien's own characteristics and the characteristics of his employer. Multiple regression analysis is used to relate the wages of the alien to the explanatory variables. The variables used in this analysis are described in table 4-3 and the means and standard deviations of the variables are reported in table 4-4. The multiple regression analyses are reported in tables 4-5 and 4-6, which differ only in the latter's including variables for duration of employment in the current or most recent job. In these tables, columns (1) and (2) rely exclusively on the demographic data from the I-213 form, with column (1) based on the full sample and column (2) based on the subsample with employer data. A set of employer characteristics is added to the matched subsample analysis in column (3), while column (4) recomputes the equation without some variables found to be generally statistically insignificant.

(a) Structure of the Regression Equation

The regression analysis is based on the standard human capital earnings function modified for the analysis of immigrant adjustment (Chiswick, 1979; 1984). The natural logarithm of the wage is regressed on measures of labor market experience, duration of U.S.

Table 4-3

Description of Variables Used in Regression Analyses
of Wages and Employer Characteristics

Code	Description
Aliens characteristics	
WAGE, LNWAGE	Hourly wage and its natural logarithm.
YREXP, YREXPSQ	Years of "labor market experience," measured as years since age 15; the square of YREXP.
TIMEUS, TIMEUSSQ	Years in the U.S. calculated as difference between month and year of apprehension and month and year of last illegal entry; the square of TIMEUS.
NOTMAR	If person is not "married spouse present" = 1, if married spouse present = 0 .
MEXICO EUROCAN LATAMER ASIA/AFRI	Country of citizenship—Mexico (benchmark); Europe and Canada; other Latin America and Caribbean; Asia, Africa and Other.
EWI STUDENT VISITOR	Status at entry—Entry without inspection (benchmark); student visa; visitor visa and small number of other visas.
JOBTENURE, JOBTENSQ	Years working for the current or most recent employer calculated as the difference between month and year employment ended (or date of apprehension of currently employed) and month and year employment started. The square of JOBTENURE.
NOTCURR	Dichotomous variable equal to unity if not employed at time of apprehension (i.e., wages refer to recent rather than current employment).
Employers Characteristics	
MANUF REST SERVICE	Industry of employment—Manufacturing and construction (benchmark); restaurant; other service.
Employers Characteristics	
MSTCOMSK	Skill level of most common male nonsupervisory job—Skilled (professional, administrative, technical craft or skilled production) = 1; Unskilled (operative, service, handler, agriculture) = 0.

Table 4-3 (Continued)

Code	Description
Employers Characteristics	
UNION	Union membership among nonsupervisory workers (percent).
NOHSWAGE, HSWAGE, COLWAGE	Average hourly wage paid to those who did not graduate from high school, to high school graduates (without college), and to college graduates. (For a typical 25-year-old male with two years work experience with the establishment.)
SUBBR	Type of ownership—Subsidiary or Branch=1, Otherwise=0.
IMMIGHIRE	Recent immigrants among persons hired in past year (percent).
SIZE	Number of employees.
PVTOWN	Privately owned establishment (proprietorship, partnership or family held corporation)=1, otherwise=0.
SEASONAL	Seasonal patterns in employment=1, no seasonality=0.
LOWEDUC	Employees with less than a high school degree (percent).
FORMAL	Newly hired employees recruited by formal methods (percent).
ENGSPREQ	Newly hired employees required to be able to speak English (percent).
UNIREQ	Newly hired employees required to have union membership (percent).
MINORRACE	Hispanic and Asian-origin employees (percent).
PAYDAYWK	Frequency of pay—Daily or weekly=1, less often=0.
LEGALIMM	Newly hired immigrants who entered the U.S. legally (percent).
CURRIMM	Recent immigrants (immigrated within the last 5 years) among employees (percentage).
ORIGINSM	Employees of same race-ethnic origin as the illegal alien (percent).
DEPORT	Any illegal alien employee deported in last year = 1, otherwise=0.
HSPOWN	Hispanic ownership: Hispanic=1, non-Hispanic or nonfamily held corporation = 0.

residence, marital status, and country of origin. Years of schooling, an important variable for most analyses of earnings, is not available in the data. Job tenure and method of illegal entry recorded from the I-213 and employer characteristics from the establishment survey, variables not available in analyses for the foreign born using census and other survey data, are included in the analysis.

The I-213 includes data on the illegal aliens' earnings per unit of time from the current or most recent employer. As with most survey or administrative data, ambiguities arise as to whether the wage data are net or gross of payroll taxes and other deductions, and as to whether the data include tips or other supplemental compensation (e.g., free meals). It is assumed that the aliens consistently reported gross earnings, excluding nonpecuniary supplements. Most of the aliens reported hourly wage rates. For those who reported their earnings on some other basis, such as a day or week, standard daily or weekly hours based on the assumption of full-time employment was used to convert to an hourly wage rate.

In most labor market surveys, data are not available on the respondent's actual number of years of labor market experience. It is, however, generally assumed that adult men have been in the labor force continuously since leaving school. Then, if it is assumed that schooling starts at age five and that one year of schooling is completed for each year of attendance, it has become customary to measure the number of years of potential labor market experience as age minus years of schooling minus five years. Unfortunately, with the absence of data on years of schooling it is not possible to use this technique. For this study, labor market experience is measured by the number of years since age 15 (YREXP). This may actually be the most appropriate measure. Illegal aliens tend to have low levels of formal schooling. For example, the schooling level in the North-Houstoun sample of adult illegal alien men was 5.2 years for Mexican nationals and 9.9 years for other nationals (Chiswick, 1984). Ten years of schooling would imply entry into the full-time labor force at about age 15. Labor market experience acquired prior to age 15, particularly in the country of origin, may not be very productive at older ages in the U.S.

The measure of duration of U.S. residence (TIMEUS) is the number of years and fractions of years between the date of action (i.e., when the I-213 form was completed) and the date of last entry into the illegal status. This would be the date of last entry into the U.S. for most illegal aliens, such as EWIs and those who entered with fraudulent documents. It would be later for some who entered with a valid visa and subsequently violated the conditions of the visa.

Another unique feature of the I-213 is information on the duration of employment with the current or most recent employer. This permits the explicit incorporation of variables for job tenure into the regression analysis of wages. It is hypothesized that, controlling for total and U.S. labor market experience, a longer job tenure is associated with higher earnings. This arises in part because of the positive effects on earnings of greater firm-specific training. It also arises from a better matching of workers and jobs. Where the match is poor, earnings are lower and separations (quits or lay-offs) occur sooner.

The job tenure variable (JOBTENURE) is measured from the I-213 form as the number of years (and fractions of a year) from the start to the end of the period of employment for the current or most recent employer. For those still employed at the date of apprehension, which is most of the sample, this date was used as the end point. A dichotomous variable is also created for those not currently employed (NOTCURR). Because job tenure variables are generally not available, the regression equations are reported for comparative purposes with and without these variables.

There are, therefore, three measures of labor market experience, total experience (YREXP), U.S. experience since the most recent illegal entry (TIMEUS) and job tenure (JOBTENURE). When job tenure is not in the equation, controlling for TIMEUS, the variable YREXP measures the partial effect on wages of labor market

Table 4-4

Means and Standard Deviations of Characteristics of
Apprehended Illegal Aliens, by Country of Origin

Variable	All aliens		Mexican aliens		Non-Mexican aliens	
	Full sample (1)	Sample with employer data (2)	Full sample (3)	Sample with employer data (4)	Full sample (5)	Sample with employer data (6)
Aliens characteristics						
WAGE	4.523 (1.813)	4.603 (1.707)	4.417 (1.613)	4.443 (1.570)	4.733 (2.147)	4.889 (1.907)
LNWAGE	1.440 (.368)	1.467 (.340)	1.424 (.351)	1.438 (.323)	1.472 (.398)	1.520 (.364)
YREXP	15.566 (9.164)	15.549 (9.145)	14.050 (8.440)	13.479 (7.732)	18.484 (9.822)	19.164 (10.294)
TIMEUS	3.420 (3.207)	3.518 (3.235)	3.434 (3.299)	3.416 (3.406)	3.391 (3.032)	3.701 (2.918)
NOTMAR	0.545 (.499)	0.551 (.499)	0.524 (.501)	0.558 (.499)	0.585 (.495)	0.537 (.502)
MEXICO	0.663 (.474)	0.642 (.481)	1.000 (.000)	1.000 (.000)	0.000 (.000)	0.000 (.000)
EUROCAN	0.068 (.252)	0.070 (.255)	0.000 (.000)	0.000 (.000)	0.202 (.404)	0.194 (.398)
LATAMER	0.201 (.401)	0.225 (.418)	0.000 (.000)	0.000 (.000)	0.596 (.493)	0.627 (.487)

Table 4-4 (Continued)

Variable	All aliens		Mexican aliens		Non-Mexican aliens	
	Full sample	Sample with employer data	Full sample	Sample with employer data	Full sample	Sample with employer data
	(1)	(2)	(3)	(4)	(5)	(6)
ASIA/AFRI	0.068	0.064	0.000	0.000	0.202	0.179
	(.252)	(.246)	(.000)	(.000)	(.404)	(.386)
EWI	0.799	0.791	0.962	0.958	0.479	0.493
	(.401)	(.407)	(.191)	(.201)	(.502)	(.504)
STUDENT	0.011	0.016	0.000	0.000	0.032	0.045
	(1.03)	(.126)	(.000)	(.000)	(.177)	(.208)
VISITOR	0.190	0.193	0.038	0.042	0.489	0.463
	(.393)	(.395)	(.191)	(.201)	(.503)	(.502)
JOBTENURE	1.816	1.918	1.845	1.847	1.763	2.037
	(2.322)	(2.411)	(2.395)	(2.346)	(2.194)	(2.346)
NOTCURR	0.079	0.088	0.059	0.074	0.114	0.111
	(0.270)	(0.284)	(0.236)	(0.264)	(0.320)	(0.317)
Employers Characteristics						
UNION	n.a.	29.306	n.a.	25.313	n.a.	33.001
		(42.722)		(41.213)		(44.180)
SIZE	n.a.	157.212	n.a.	160.450	n.a.	155.731
		(305.751)		(347.132)		(232.019)
HSWAGE	n.a.	5.947	n.a.	5.816	n.a.	6.001
		(2.188)		(2.117)		(2.147)

Table 4-4 (Continued)

	All aliens		Mexican aliens		Non-Mexican aliens	
	Full sample	Sample with employer data	Full sample	Sample with employer data	Full sample	Sample with employer data
Variable	(1)	(2)	(3)	(4)	(5)	(6)
MSTCOMSK	n.a.	0.109 (.312)	n.a.	0.091 (.289)	n.a.	0.139 (.348)
SUBBR	n.a.	0.275 (.447)	n.a.	0.283 (.453)	n.a.	0.254 (.438)
REST	n.a.	0.295 (.457)	n.a.	0.333 (.473)	n.a.	0.239 (.430)
SERVICE	n.a.	0.321 (.468)	n.a.	0.317 (.467)	n.a.	0.313 (.467)
MANUF	n.a.	0.383 (.487)	n.a.	0.350 (.479)	n.a.	0.448 (.501)
IMMIGHIRE	n.a.	0.215 (.289)	n.a.	0.204 (.290)	n.a.	0.253 (.293)
Number of observations[a]	292	193	185	120	107	73

a. Indicates the maximum number of observations. Because of missing values, samples may be smaller for particular variables.

n.a. = Not applicable.

Table 4-5

Regression Analysis of Wages for Apprehended Illegal Aliens
(Dependent Variable: Natural Logarithm of the Hourly Wage)

Variable	Full sample[a] (1)	Sample with employer data (2)[a]	(3)	(4)
YREXP	0.021 (2.433)	0.014 (1.427)	0.019 (1.953)	0.019 (2.219)
YREXPSQ[b]	-4.432 (-2.235)	-2.782 (-1.286)	-3.410 (-1.618)	-3.237 (-1.688)
TIMEUS	0.082 (5.135)	0.069 (3.725)	0.040 (2.126)	0.041 (2.371)
TIMEUSSQ	-0.004 (-2.642)	-0.002 (-1.244)	-0.001 (-0.921)	-0.002 (-1.154)
NOTMAR	-0.033 (-0.744)	-0.013 (-0.277)	0.005 (0.096)	n.a.
EUROCAN	0.098 (0.849)	0.201 (1.617)	0.091 (0.743)	n.a.
LATAMER	-0.053 (-1.049)	-0.039 (-0.725)	-0.035 (-0.664)	n.a.
ASIA/AFRI	-0.138 (-1.188)	0.113 (0.843)	0.045 (0.338)	n.a.
STUDENT	-0.148 (-0.680)	-0.436 (-2.009)	-0.307 (-1.522)	-0.251 (-1.701)
VISITOR	0.132 (1.528)	0.076 (0.846)	0.050 (0.566)	0.075 (1.348)
UNION[b]	n.a.	n.a.	11.273 (1.895)	13.835 (2.695)
SIZE[b]	n.a.	n.a.	0.007 (0.096)	n.a.
HSWAGE[b]	n.a.	n.a.	2.051 (1.641)	2.417 (2.178)
MSTCOMSK	n.a.	n.a.	0.162 (2.154)	0.189 (2.800)
SUBBR	n.a.	n.a.	0.048 (0.913)	n.a.
REST	n.a.	n.a.	-0.162 (-2.613)	-0.157 (-2.761)

Table 4-5 (Continued)

Variable	Full sample[a] (1)	Sample with employer data (2)[a]	(3)	(4)
SERVICE	n.a.	n.a.	-0.071 (-1.302)	-0.069 (-1.417)
IMMIGHIRE[b]	n.a.	n.a.	-5.109 (-0.687)	n.a.
R^2	.277	.346	.490	.485
Adjusted R^2	.249	.309	.425	.449
No. of obser.	272	184	160	170

NOTE: Benchmark is an illegal alien who entered the U.S. without inspection: in column (1), (2), and (3) is from Mexico; in column (3) and (4) works in the manufacturing industry.

a. Accept the null hypothesis of identical structures between illegal aliens with and without employer data. Calculated F-value of 1.26 from the Chow-test is less than the 5 percent critical value $F(11;250;.05) = 1.83$.

b. Estimated coefficient = stated coefficient x 10^{-4}.

t-ratios are in parentheses.

n.a. denotes the variable was not included in that regression.

experience in the origin country and in previous stays in the U.S. Similarly, controlling for YREXP, the variable TIMEUS measures the *differential* effect on wages in the U.S. of current stay and previous experience. When JOBTENURE is in the equation, TIMEUS measures the differential effect of U.S. experience prior to the current or most recent job.

Other variables included in the regression analysis are dichotomous variables for marital status (NOTMAR = 1 if not married), and status at entry (STUDENT = 1 if student visa, VISITOR = 1 if visitor or other visa, with EWI as the benchmark). Country-of-origin dichotomous variables are also included with Mexico serving as the benchmark. The country groupings are Europe and Canada (EUROCAN), Latin America other than Mexico (LAT-AMER) and Asia and Africa (ASIA/AFRI). Since the dependent variable is the natural logarithm of the hourly wage, the coefficient

Table 4-6

**Regression Analysis of Wages for Apprehended Illegal Aliens,
Controlling for Job Tenure
(Dependent Variable: Natural Logarithm of the Hourly Wage)**

Variable	Full sample[a]	Sample with employer data		
	(1)	(2)[a]	(3)	(4)
JOBTENURE	0.084	0.078	0.049	0.048
	(3.190)	(2.674)	(1.538)	(1.768)
JOBTENSQ	-0.004	-0.005	-0.002	-0.002
	(-1.557)	(-1.571)	(-0.625)	(-0.821)
NOTCURR	-0.140	-0.169	-0.175	-0.151
	(-1.953)	(-2.238)	(-2.269)	(-2.141)
YREXP	0.017	0.014	0.019	0.018
	(2.136)	(1.572)	(2.013)	(2.214)
YREXPSQ[a]	-4.153	-3.626	-4.037	-3.679
	(-2.202)	(-1.713)	(-1.951)	(-1.953)
TIMEUS	0.036	0.015	0.019	0.022
	(1.904)	(1.572)	(0.853)	(1.109)
TIMEUSSQ	-0.001	0.0004	-0.0002	-0.0007
	(-0.654)	(0.213)	(-0.118)	(-0.455)
NOTMAR	-0.020	-0.010	0.013	n.a.
	(-0.484)	(-0.213)	(0.262)	
EUROCAN	0.174	0.246	0.128	n.a.
	(1.568)	(2.058)	(1.082)	
LATAMER	-0.017	-0.005	0.007	n.a.
	(-0.357)	(-0.100)	(0.138)	
ASIA/AFRI	-0.059	0.142	0.106	n.a.
	(-0.528)	(1.109)	(0.846)	
STUDENT	-0.286	-0.499	-0.415	-0.295
	(-1.340)	(-2.372)	(-2.130)	(-2.074)
VISITOR	0.064	0.047	0.003	0.060
	(0.771)	(0.540)	(0.033)	(1.152)
UNION[a]	n.a.	n.a.	4.513	7.478
			(0.792)	(1.494)
SIZE[a]	n.a.	n.a.	0.036	n.a.
			(0.051)	
HSWAGE[a]	n.a.	n.a.	3.761	4.369
			(3.007)	(3.850)

Table 4-6 (Continued)

| Variable | Full sample[a] | Sample with employer data | | |
	(1)	(2)[a]	(3)	(4)
MSTCOMSK	n.a.	n.a.	0.177 (2.289)	0.195 (2.827)
SUBBR	n.a.	n.a.	0.063 (1.153)	n.a.
RESTAUR	n.a.	n.a.	-0.129 (-2.088)	-0.129 (-2.300)
SERVICE	n.a.	n.a.	-0.050 (-0.901)	-0.052 (-1.074)
IMMIGHIRE[a]	n.a.	n.a.	-2.046 (-0.287)	n.a.
R^2	.354	.422	.562	.552
ADJ. R^2	.321	.377	.453	.517
No. of obser.	270	181	155	166

NOTE: Benchmark is an illegal alien who entered the U.S. without inspection: in columns (1), (2), and (3) is from Mexico; in columns (3) and (4) works in the manufacturing industry.

a. Estimated coefficient $=$ stated coefficient x 10^{-4}

t-ratios are in parentheses.

n.a. denotes the variable was not included in the regression.

of a dichotomous variable may be interpreted as approximately the percentage difference in earnings due to that characteristic. The approximation is more exact the closer to zero is the estimated coefficient.

(b) Estimated Equation—Aliens' Characteristics

The regression equations in columns (1) and (2) of table 4-5 are for the full sample and the subsample of illegal aliens with employer survey data. A Chow-test was performed to test the null hypothesis that there is no significant difference between the coefficients in the subsample for which there are no employer data and the subsample with employer data. The test indicated that the null hypothesis cannot be rejected (calculated F-value $= 1.26$; the 5 percent critical

F-value $F(11;250; .05) = 1.83$). That is, the two samples are consistent with the hypothesis that they are drawn from the same population.[2]

For the full sample, wages rise significantly but at a decreasing rate with experience in the country of origin (YREXP) and with duration of U.S. residence (TIMEUS) (table 4-5, column 1). In the full sample, the partial effect on U.S. wages of an extra year of preimmigration experience is 1.2 percent when evaluated at 10 years of labor market experience (YREXP=10). This is about the same as in census data on the foreign born. An extra year in the U.S. rather than in the country of origin raises earnings by 5.5 percent when evaluated at the mean duration of 3.4 years.

The regression equations suggest that relative to the benchmark, Mexico, there are no country-of-origin wage differences, holding constant the illegal aliens' experience and demographic characteristics, except for 20 percent higher earnings for illegal aliens from Europe/Canada in the sample with employer data (table 4-5, column 2). When the method-of-entry variables are deleted, the European/Canadian origin variable is highly significant and the coefficient implies about 20 to 25 percent higher earnings for European/Canadian illegal aliens.[3] Nearly all of the European/Canadian illegal aliens had violated a visitor visa.

It will be shown below that the significantly higher earnings of the European/Canadian illegal aliens relative to those from Mexico disappear when employer characteristics are held constant. The earnings advantage of European/Canadian illegal aliens arises from their being more successful in obtaining jobs with employers who offer higher wages. They are more likely to be employed in unionized, higher wage structure, manufacturing establishments. This may reflect unmeasured dimensions of their higher level of skill, including formal schooling, fluency in English, and a greater transferability of their skills to the U.S. labor market.

There does not appear to be a significant effect of marital status on earnings. The absence of a marital status effect might seem surprising since being married is generally associated with a large and highly significant positive effect on earnings for the native and foreign born in census and survey data. Married men may earn more than single men because they make greater investments in labor market training, rather than because of innate ability or health. If so, the estimated earnings differences would be smaller or nonexistent for a young population, such as the one under study, that is currently making investments in on-the-job training. Alternatively, there may be a different effect of marital status on the selection criteria for migration among illegal aliens. Favorable self-selection, in terms of ability, motivation and health status, may be more intense among single men than among married men in an illegal alien population. For example, if men who have less ability or ambition or who are in poorer health are less likely to marry, among nonmigrants single men would have lower earnings. Among migrants, however, the single men may be the most highly motivated for their own economic advancement and may have the weakest family ties in the origin. Hence, they may have made greater investments specific to the U.S. labor market.

The data suggest lower earnings among those who entered with a student visa (STUDENT) compared with those who entered without inspection.[4] This may reflect the smaller set of wage opportunities available to those who combine schooling and work (Lazear, 1977), or a smaller amount of actual U.S. labor market experience for the same number of years in the U.S.

The regression equations in table 4-6 repeat those in table 4-5 but include the job tenure variables. Adding these variables to the regression equation systematically increases the model's explanatory power. Controlling for total and U.S. labor market experience, earnings rise at a decreasing rate with duration of employment on the current job. When evaluated at the mean job tenure of 1.8 years, an extra year of experience with the same employer raises earnings by 7 to 8 percent (table 4-6 columns (1) and (2)) over the effect of working for another U.S. employer. Controlling for employer characteristics (columns (3) and (4)), the partial effect of job tenure when evaluated at the mean falls to 4.5 percent. The strong effect on wages of current employer experience may arise from greater firm-specific training and from longer job tenures when there is a better match of worker skills and job characteristics.

About 8 percent of the sample reported wages for a job that ended prior to the date of apprehension. These workers reported about 15 percent lower wages when other variables are the same. Part of this differential arises from the time gap between the end of employment and the apprehension. Perhaps more important may be the reverse causation—those who received lower wages because of lower productivity or a poorer job match are more likely to be without a current job.

When job tenure and current employment are held constant, the partial effects of some of the other explanatory variables are altered. The most important change is the sharp decline in the partial effect of U.S. labor market experience. The two variables JOBTENURE and TIMEUS are highly correlated ($R = 0.58$), in part because the former is generally bounded by the latter.[5] Note, however, the change in the interpretation of TIMEUS when job tenure is held constant. It now measures the differential effect on earnings of U.S. experience prior to joining the current employer.

The effect of an extra year of experience on U.S. wages at an establishment is greatest if the experience is with the establishment, less so if it is with another U.S. employer and least if it is preimmigration experience. That is, the effect of experience on the wages of illegal aliens is greatest the more recent it is and the more transferable it is to the current employer.

(c) A Comparison with the North-Houstoun Sample

The North-Houstoun sample of male apprehended illegal aliens may be used to test the robustness of the findings in the analysis of the wages of illegal aliens. The North-Houstoun sample was taken in 1975, was nationwide, included a variable for years of schooling completed (EDUC) and included several measures of wages, but had no data on employer characteristics. Because of a large number of missing values, only about 400 observations are available when schooling is included in the analysis.

Using the same regression methodology, table 4-7 reports the results for three dependent variables, total earnings in 1974 (EARN), U.S. earnings in 1974 (USER), and hourly pay in the most recent (1975) U.S. job (HRPA). Since the dependent variables are expressed in natural logarithms, comparisons of coefficients can be made across the equations and with the more recent Chicago survey. The data indicate a small, although highly statistically significant, effect of an extra year of schooling on earnings for illegal aliens. It is 3.9 percent for annual total earnings, 3.2 percent for annual U.S. earnings, and 2.3 percent for the U.S. hourly wage. By way of comparison, in census data the partial effect of schooling on weekly earnings is about 5 percent for the foreign born and 7 percent for the native born.

Table 4-7

Regression Analysis of Earnings for
Apprehended Illegal Aliens, 1975[a]
(North-Houstoun sample)

Variable[b]	Dependent variable		
	LNEARN[c]	LNUSER[c]	LNHRPA[c]
EDUC	.03852	.03249	.02295
	(2.97)	(2.60)	(3.41)
YREXP	.04354	.03077	.02383
	(3.32)	(2.43)	(3.51)
YREXPSQ	-.00077	-.00054	-.00049
	(-2.85)	(-2.06)	(-3.51)
TIMEUS	.06991	.07554	.06437
	(2.21)	(2.48)	(4.47)
TIMEUSSQ	-.00370	-.00338	-.00272
	(-1.70)	(-1.61)	(-2.60)
LNWW	.85246	1.01081	d
	(16.62)	(20.72)	
EUROCAN	.35274	.36515	.35526
	(2.10)	(2.26)	(4.09)
ASIA/AFRI	-.02860	-.02634	.02141
	(-0.17)	(-0.16)	(0.24)

Table 4-7 (Continued)

Variable[b]	Dependent variable		
	LNEARN[c]	LNUSER[c]	LNHRPA[c]
CARIB	-.08138	-.02262	-.00611
	(-0.68)	(-0.20)	(-0.10)
SOAMER	-.05855	-.01512	-.01897
	(-0.46)	(-0.12)	(-0.29)
WESTCO	-.15385	-.09766	-.10567
	(-1.50)	(-0.99)	(-2.00)
SWBORD	-.33647	-.44454	-.22448
	(-2.98)	(-4.09)	(-3.84)
CONSTANT	-.19222	-.71589	.55667
	(-0.80)	(-3.09)	(5.30)
R^2	.60628	.69671	.31100
Adj. R^2	.59426	.68745	.29176
Number of observations	406	406	406

SOURCE: David North and Marion Houstoun, microdata file on apprehended illigal aliens, 1975.

a. Men age 16 and over who worked in the U.S. for at least two weeks during their most recent stay.

b. EDUC is years of schooling; YREXP and YREXPSQ are years of labor market experience and its square; LNWW is the log of weeks worked; TIMEUS and TIMEUSSQ are total number of years of U.S. experience and its square; WESTCO and SWBORD are west coast and southwest border, respectively. Country categories are Mexico (benchmark), Europe and Canada (EURCAN), Asia and Africa (ASIA/AFRI), the Caribbean (CARIB) and Central and South America (SOAMER).

c. LNEARN is natural logarithm of annual earnings in 1975, LNUSER is logarithm of U.S. earnings in 1975, LNHRPA is logarithm of hourly pay in the U.S. Annual earnings expressed in hundreds of dollars.

d. Variable not entered.

t-ratios in parentheses.

In the North-Houstoun sample, an extra year of premigration labor market experience (evaluated at 10 years and controlling for weeks worked) raises earnings by about 2.8 percent for total annual earnings, 2.0 percent for U.S. annual earnings and 1.4 percent for hourly earnings. The larger coefficients for schooling and experience when total annual earnings is the dependent variable implies that illegal aliens with more schooling and more experience in the country of origin work more hours per week in the U.S.

The partial effect of experience in the hourly wage equations, when evaluated at 10 years, is 1.2 percent in the Chicago survey (table 4-5), and is 1.4 percent in the North-Houstoun data. The difference is remarkably small.

Recall that an extra year of U.S. labor market experience in the Chicago survey raised wages by 5.5 percent when evaluated at 3.4 years, the mean duration in these data (table 4-5). When evaluated at this same value, an extra year of U.S. experience in the North-Houstoun data raised annual earnings by 4.5 percent, U.S. earnings by 5.3 percent and U.S. hourly earnings by 5.6 percent. The differences between the Chicago and North-Houstoun coefficients are very small and not statistically significant.

Even after controlling for years of schooling and lower earnings on the West Coast and especially along the southwestern border, the North-Houstoun data show a pattern of earnings differences by country of origin. Other things the same, European/Canadian illegal aliens earn significantly more than Mexican illegal aliens, although there are no differences between Mexican and other illegal aliens. The coefficient for European/Canadians is larger in the North-Houstoun data (about 40 percent higher wages) than in the Chicago survey (about 25 percent higher wages). The difference may be reflecting the effects on wages of unmeasured differences in their location.

The large regional differences in wages in the North-Houstoun data are striking. Controlling for schooling, total labor market experience, duration in the U.S. and country of origin, wages for illegal aliens are much lower (20 to 30 percent lower) along the southwestern border (SWBORD), and somewhat lower (by 10 to 15 percent) along the West Coast (WESTCO) than in the rest of the country. These regional differentials do not reflect differences in the distribution of illegal aliens by country of origin. There is a significant West Coast effect for non-Mexican aliens, but only for the hourly wage rate. All of the southwestern border observations were Mexican nationals. When the data are limited to Mexican illegal aliens, other things the same, hourly earnings are about 20 percent lower along the southwestern border and 10 percent lower along the West Coast than in the rest of the country (primarily the midwestern states).[6] The regional differences for weekly earnings (i.e., annual earnings with a statistical control for weeks worked) are even larger among the Mexican illegal aliens.

It is difficult to reconcile such large regional effects as reflecting merely differences in the cost of living. To the extent that they represent real differences in hourly wages and/or employment opportunities they would constitute compelling forces for the redistribution of Mexican illegal aliens away from these entry points to the rest of the country. It is, therefore, not surprising that the Midwest is believed to have experienced a very sharp increase in the number of Mexican and other Western Hemisphere illegal aliens in the past decade, in spite of the seemingly sluggish performance of the Midwest economy.[7] For Mexican illegal aliens it was still an area of outstanding opportunities.

(d) Adding Employer Characteristics to the Equation

Previous labor market research has shown there is a systematic relationship between employer or workplace characteristics and the wages of workers. For example, wages tend to be higher in larger establishments and where there is a union.[8] The direction of causation is ambiguous—some of the earnings advantage of workers in larger and more highly unionized establishments may reflect unmeasured dimensions of greater worker skill. Some other issues related to employee compensation have been subject to less study, such as whether wages are higher, other things the same, the greater the skill level of co-workers and whether the type of ownership of the establishment matters.

In general, it has been difficult to test hypotheses regarding the effect of establishment or workplace characteristics on the wages of workers because of the relative scarcity of data that match worker characteristics to employer or establishment characteristics. A unique feature of the illegal alien survey is that worker and establishment characteristics are matched for a sample of nearly 200 observations. The illegal aliens for whom the matched data are available do not seem to differ in any material way from the other illegal aliens in the full sample.

This section augments the regression analysis of illegal alien wages by adding to the earnings function several variables describing the establishment's characteristics. These variables are defined in table 4-3.

One variable is the size of the establishment, as measured by the number of employees (SIZE). Tests during the development of the survey instrument indicated that the respondents could reliably report the number of employees, but not any other measure of size, such as value added. The type of ownership of the establishment is treated as a dichotomous variable, where SUBBR=1 if it is a branch or subsidiary of a larger enterprise, and SUBBR=0 if it is an independent establishment.

Dichotomous variables are also included for the type of industry, where REST and SERVICE designate restaurant and other service establishments, respectively, with manufacturing as the benchmark. It is hypothesized that industrial characteristics influence reported wage rates, with wages being lower in the restaurant sector where some tip income and in-kind income in the form of free meals may not be included in the reported wage. It has also been suggested that there is less industry-specific and firm-specific training in most restaurant jobs and that this is particularly attractive for illegal alien workers (Piore, 1979 and Bailey, 1985). If so, there would be a flatter experience earnings profile for the restaurant sector; new workers would have higher wages but more experienced workers would receive lower wages.

Several establishment characteristics that describe co-workers are also included in the equation. One is the degree of unionization of the workforce, as measured by the proportion of nonsupervisory workers who are union members (UNION).[9] Two others describe the skills of workers. A wage scale variable is the average wage paid to a hypothetical 25-year-old high school graduate who has worked for the establishment for two years (HSWAGE). The other is the skill level of the most common male nonsupervisory job (MST-COMSK). It is treated as a dichotomous variable which takes the value unity if this job is an administrative, professional, technical craft or skilled production job, and is zero if it is an operative, service, handler, or agricultural job. It is hypothesized that UNION, HSWAGE and MSTCOMSK all have positive effects on the illegal alien's wage.

There is much interest in the extent to which illegal aliens work within an immigrant or ethnic enclave and the effect, if any, of ethnic enclave employment on their wages and job mobility. It is often speculated that ethnic enclave establishments pay lower wages, perhaps because the workers they hire have less job mobility and fewer skills, even after controlling statistically for readily measured dimensions of skill. Indeed, it is often said that illegal aliens are locked into low-paying ethnic enclave establishments because of a fear of being reported to the immigration authorities. Perhaps as temporary workers they prefer jobs that utilize the skills, including language skills, of the country of origin, and avoid jobs that require investments specific to the U.S. Alternatively, for relatively new immigrants, whether legal or illegal, ethnic enclave employment may serve a transitional or "half-way house" function where some of the skills specific to their country of origin have greater "transferability" than in the general labor market. Foreign language fluency may be the most obvious country-of-origin skills that are more highly rewarded in the enclave than outside.

The degree of ethnic enclave employment is measured by the proportion of recent immigrants (i.e., immigrants in the U.S. five or fewer years) among workers hired in the past year (IMMIGHIRE). Because of the potentially offsetting effects of the several hypotheses regarding this variable, there is no unambiguous prediction as to the sign of its coefficient in the wage equation.

The means and standard deviations of the establishment variables are reported in table 4-4, overall, and separately for the Mexican and non-Mexican illegal aliens. The Mexican illegal aliens work in larger establishments (SIZE is larger by about 3 percent), but they are less likely to be unionized, and have a slightly lower skill level for the most common male nonsupervisory job. There is little difference in type of ownership, over one-quarter work in subsidiary or branch establishments. The Mexican illegal aliens work in establishments that have a smaller proportion of recent immigrants among those hired in the past year, 20 percent compared with 25 percent for the others.

The establishment characteristics are added to the regression equation for wages in table 4-5 column (3). Several of the variables in the equation, some measuring the alien's characteristics and others measuring the establishment's characteristics, are not statistically significant. Deleting several of the insignificant variables, the equation is re-estimated in table 4-5 column (4). Because of missing values for some variables in the establishment data, the sample size increases when certain variables are deleted from the regression equation.

There is a significant positive relationship between the wages of the illegal aliens and the degree of unionization (UNION). Going from a 0 percent to 100 percent unionization, for example, raises the hourly wage of the illegal alien, other things the same, by about 11 to 14 percent. This is on the same order of magnitude as the measured effects of unions on wages in industry and general population studies (Lewis, 1983 and Freeman, 1984).

Other things the same, wages are about 16 to 19 percent higher when the illegal alien works in an establishment in which the most common male nonsupervisory job is skilled (MSTCOMSK). To some extent this variable may be reflecting unmeasured dimensions of the alien's own skill, such as a higher level of schooling or being a highly skilled worker. Wages are also higher the greater the rate of pay of a "standardized worker" (HSWAGE). This may be reflecting interestablishment differences in money wage levels. Although all of the establishments are located in the Chicago SMSA, there may be local area differences in wages, perhaps reflecting transportation costs, or interestablishment differentials for other nonpecuniary aspects of the job, even when the major industry category is held constant.

The wages of illegal aliens are significantly lower in the restaurant sector than in manufacturing. Part of this 16 percent differential may compensate for unmeasured dimensions of job-related income, such as tips and in-kind income in the form of free meals. There is no significant difference in wages between the other service jobs and manufacturing jobs.

The wages of illegal aliens are apparently not related to the size or type of ownership of the establishment; both SIZE and SUBBR have very low t-ratios. That is, controlling for proxies for the skill level and wage structure of the establishment, as well as the illegal alien's characteristics, there is no direct independent effect on the alien's wages of either size or type of ownership of the establishment.

The extent to which recent immigrants were among those hired in the past year (IMMIGHIRE) is apparently unrelated to the illegal alien's wages. That is, other things the same, working in an establishment that hires relatively more recent immigrants does not depress the wages of illegal aliens. Thus, the ethnic enclave patterns of employment (discussed in greater detail below) do not appear to depress the wages of illegal aliens.

Total labor market experience, U.S. experience and firm-specific experience are highly significant variables, even when establishment characteristics are held constant (table 4-5 and 4-6). Note, however, that the partial effects of U.S. and firm-specific experience are lower when the establishment's characteristics are included in the equation. With a longer duration of residence there is a tendency for illegal aliens to obtain employment in higher wage establishments (higher wage structure, more highly unionized, higher skill level). Hourly wages are significantly lower (by more than 20 percent) for those who entered the U.S. under a student visa, when the statistically insignificant variables are deleted from the equation. This may reflect the narrower range of job opportunities that are available for those combining schooling and work.

In summary, the hourly wages of the apprehended illegal aliens are significantly related to their individual characteristics and the characteristics of their employers. Wages are higher for those with more preimmigration labor market experience, who have been in the U.S. longer, who worked for their current employer a longer period of time, and who did not enter the U.S. with a student visa. The wages of illegal aliens are also higher the greater the degree of unionization, the higher the wage structure of the employer, and the higher the skill level of the employer's most common male nonsupervisory job. Money wages are lower in the restaurant sector than in manufacturing and other services.

These findings suggest that establishments that are more highly unionized, have a higher wage structure, and have a more highly skilled workforce may be hiring and retaining the more productive illegal aliens, that is, they engage in "creaming."

This hypothesis can be tested by analyzing employment patterns as a function of the illegal alien's labor market experience. Of course, a positive relation between the duration in the U.S. and more favorable employer characteristics would reflect the beneficial effects of more time for job search and better information networks, as well as more narrowly defined concepts of skill.

III. Employer Characteristics

The empirical analysis of wages suggests the importance of employer characteristics to the earnings of illegal aliens. Employer characteristics are not necessarily determined independently of the alien's own characteristics. This section is concerned with the variation in employer characteristics among the apprehended illegal aliens. The analysis focuses on two types of explanatory variables. One is labor market experience, measured by the number of years since age 15 (YREXP) and the number of years in the U.S. (TIMEUS). The other is country of origin.[10] The purpose of the analysis is to determine the extent to which employer characteristics, such as size of establishment, extent of unionization and wage level, vary systematically with the alien's labor market experience and country of origin.[11] The regression equations are reported in table 4-8.

(a) Effect of Duration of Residence

The industrial characteristics of the employer vary systematically with the illegal alien's duration of residence in the country. Controlling for age and country of origin, illegal aliens who have been in the U.S. longer (TIMEUS) tend to work in larger and more highly unionized establishments (SIZE, UNION) and are more likely to be in the manufacturing sector (MANUF) (table 4-8).[12] The establishment is more likely to be a branch or subsidiary (SUBBR) than to be independently owned and operated. Illegal aliens are less likely to work for a sole proprietorship or partnership the longer their duration in the U.S.

The wage and skill level of their co-workers also varies with duration of residence. The longer they have been in the U.S. the more likely are illegal aliens to be working in establishments with higher wage structures (NOHSWAGE, HSWAGE, COLWAGE), and in which the most common male nonsupervisory job is skilled (MSTCOMSK). This may reflect the selection of more skilled or more "Americanized" illegal alien workers by employers who offer higher wages within occupational levels or who have a higher average skill level in their workforce. It may also reflect the job search benefits from greater labor market information due to a longer exposure to the U.S. labor market. On the other hand, a greater duration of U.S. residence has no significant relationship

Table 4-8

Analysis of Employer Characteristics
of Apprehended Illegal Aliens

Explanatory variables	Dependent variables				
	SIZE	UNION	MANUF	FORMAL	SUBBR
YREXP	-3.727 (-1.330)	-0.256 (-0.648)	0.006 (1.398)	-0.036 (-0.123)	-0.001 (-0.189)
TIMEUS	30.808 (4.229)	3.369 (3.302)	0.045 (4.123)	0.894 (1.196)	0.037 (3.441)
EUROCAN	200.933 (2.159)	33.177 (2.557)	0.432 (3.111)	7.631 (0.810)	0.030 (0.217)
LATAMER	-67.274 (-1.253)	3.197 (0.421)	0.015 (0.189)	5.059 (0.929)	-0.030 (-0.377)
ASIA/AFRI	79.558 (0.866)	-3.063 (-0.239)	-0.127 (-0.925)	1.929 (0.208)	-0.110 -0.808
R^2	.120	.095	.199	.017	.074
Adjusted R^2	.096	.069	.177	-.012	.048
No. of observations	184	180	184	177	184

Table 4-8 (Continued)

Explanatory variables	Dependent variables				
	ENGSPREQ	UNIREQ	MINORRACE	LOWEDUC	NOHSWAGE
YREXP	-0.122 (-0.293)	0.300 (1.626)	0.197 (0.729)	0.482 (1.401)	-0.085 (-0.049)
TIMEUS	1.014 (0.937)	0.562 (1.176)	-0.597 (-0.849)	-0.456 (-0.614)	19.460 (4.310)
EUROCAN	-8.425 (-0.619)	0.074 (0.012)	-24.078 (-2.681)	-10.161 (-0.784)	186.341 (3.342)
LATAMER	8.492 (1.078)	-7.048 (-2.026)	0.354 (0.068)	-9.242 (-1.588)	-24.027 (-0.720)
ASIA/AFRI	40.920 (3.051)	-3.776 (-0.637)	-11.376 (-1.284)	-36.508 (-4.240)	-66.408 (-1.168)
R^2	.066	.059	.048	.132	.190
Adjusted R^2	.039	.031	.022	.097	.165
No. of observations	176	177	184	128	171

Table 4-8 (Continued)

Explanatory variables	Dependent variables						
	HSWAGE	COLWAGE	MSTCOMSK	SEASONAL	PAYDAYWK	IMMIGHIRE
YREXP	-0.922 (-0.480)	0.716 (0.182)	0.000063 (0.022)	0.002 (0.405)	0.006 (1.589)	-0.176 (-0.611)
TIMEUS	21.464 (4.360)	27.822 (2.930)	0.013 (1.713)	-0.013 (-1.098)	-0.002 (-0.199)	-0.106 (-0.143)
EUROCAN	229.045 (3.601)	241.154 (1.997)	0.057 (0.596)	-0.253 (-1.622)	-0.142 (-1.130)	7.971 (0.855)
LATAMER	-14.684 (-0.402)	40.399 (0.562)	-0.027 (-0.489)	-0.230 (-2.564)	-0.092 (-1.259)	8.197 (1.479)
ASIA/AFRI	-85.341 (-1.348)	-17.996 (-0.157)	0.156 (1.648)	-0.136 (-0.884)	-0.464 (-3.729)	-6.460 (-0.704)
R^2	.188	.096	.038	.050	.078	.023
Adjusted R^2	.164	.066	.012	.023	.052	-.006
No. of observations	173	159	184	184	183	172

Table 4-8 (Continued)

Explanatory variables	Dependent variables					
	LEGALIMM	CURRIMM	ORIGINSM	DEPORT	PVTOWN	HSPOWN
YREXP	0.161 (0.329)	-0.237 (-1.152)	0.319 (1.168)	-0.002 (-1.072)	0.005 (1.138)	-0.001 (-0.528)
TIMEUS	-0.564 (-0.474)	-0.697 (-1.320)	-0.254 (-0.360)	0.009 (1.591)	-0.023 (-1.994)	-0.0004 (-0.763)
EUROCAN	11.689 (0.922)	10.668 (1.573)	6.898 (0.764)	-0.033 (-0.488)	0.025 (0.171)	-0.047 (-0.781)
LATAMER	-9.355 (-1.143)	3.814 (0.967)	-5.341 (-1.026)	-0.008 (-0.210)	-0.025 (-0.293)	-0.056 (-1.599)
ASIA/AFRI	3.028 (0.216)	-6.660 (-1.018)	-19.819 (-2.156)	-0.043 (-0.644)	-0.221 (-1.519)	-0.053 (-0.884)
R^2	.043	.054	.044	.024	.035	.030
Adjusted R^2	-.013	.025	.017	-.004	.008	.003
No. of observations	92	169	183	184	184	184

NOTES: Entries are regression coefficients, with t-ratios in parentheses.

Benchmark is an illegal alien from Mexico. Sample sizes vary because of incomplete reporting of employer characteristics. Maximum potential sample size equals 184.

with whether the alien works for an establishment that uses formal recruiting methods (FORMAL) or the degree of seasonality (SEASONAL) in employment.

The data can be used to test whether ethnic enclave patterns of employment diminish with duration of residence for illegal aliens. There is no statistically significant relation between duration of residence and several establishment characteristics, including the extent to which workers are required at the time of hire to speak English (ENGSPREQ), the proportion of Hispanics and Asians among the workforce (MINORRACE), the proportion of immigrants among recent hires (IMMIGHIRE), the proportion of immigrants in the nonsupervisory workforce (CURRIMM), or whether the other employees are of the same ethnic origin (ORIGINSM).

These patterns indicate that the degree of ethnic enclave employment in this sample of apprehended illegal aliens does not diminish with duration of residence. Perhaps there were too few long-duration illegal aliens for there to be noticeable effects on ethnic enclave employment.[13] Alternatively, since employment in the ethnic enclave does not have a depressing effect on wages, there may be no particular incentive for a change in the degree of ethnic enclave employment with duration of residence.

(b) Effect of Premigration Experience

Controlling for duration in the U.S., the number of years since age 15 (YREXP) measures labor market experience prior to the most recent episode as an illegal alien. When duration in the U.S. and country of origin are held constant, premigration experience appears to be generally unrelated to the employer characteristics considered in this analysis (table 4-8). One possible exception is a marginally significant tendency for the employers of older illegal aliens to be more likely to pay workers daily or weekly rather than less frequently (biweekly, monthly). This may be an index of a lower quality job, but in the absence of other significant effects it may merely be the consequence of random sampling. Other studies of legal and illegal aliens also show a much weaker effect of premigration experience on labor market outcomes than is the case for postmigration experience (Chiswick 1979, 1984).

(c) Effects of Country of Origin

The data can be used to explore differences in employer characteristics by country of origin. Some striking patterns emerge.

Compared with Mexican illegal aliens, European and Canadian illegal aliens are more likely to work in larger (SIZE), more highly unionized (UNION) establishments, and are more likely to be in manufacturing (MANUF) (table 4-8).[14] The Europeans and Canadians are also more likely to work in establishments with higher wage scales. Illegal aliens from other areas do not differ from the Mexican nationals in these characteristics. These patterns may reflect the higher levels of schooling and occupational skills of illegal aliens from more highly developed source countries (Chiswick, 1984; North and Houstoun, 1976).

On the other hand, it is only the Asian/African illegal aliens who are more likely than Mexican nationals to work for employers for whom the most common male nonsupervisory job is in the skill category (MSTCOMSK). The Asian/African illegal aliens are less likely to work at an establishment the larger the proportion of workers without a high school degree (LOWEDUC). These findings suggest that the Asian/African illegal aliens have a higher skill level than those of Mexican origin.

Mexican illegal aliens are significantly more likely to work in establishments that reported seasonality in their employment (SEASONAL). The much lower cost of to-and-fro migration and illegal entry for Mexican nationals than for nationals of other countries may provide greater incentives for Mexican nationals to accept, if not prefer, seasonal employment in the U.S.[15]

Illegal aliens from Asia and Africa are less likely to work in establishments with workers of their same ethnic origin

(ORIGINSM) and are more likely to work in establishments that require a speaking knowledge of English (ENGSPREQ). Because of the relatively small numbers of Asian and African immigrants in the Chicago labor market and the heterogeneity of their origins and languages, Asian/African illegal aliens may be less able than the Hispanics or Europeans to find employment in "ethnic enclaves." It will be shown in the next chapter, which analyzes establishment characteristics, that illegal alien employers are more likely to demonstrate ethnic enclave characteristics than are randomly selected employers. They are more likely to be owned by a Hispanic and employ other Hispanic and Asian workers.

IV. Exploitation of Illegal Aliens

The popular literature contains many allegations of exploitation of illegal aliens by unscrupulous employers.[16] Exploitation is usually not defined, but is generally thought to mean either the payment of subminimum wages or the payment of wages lower than their productivity. A corollary of the existence of exploitation is that illegal aliens have little or no job mobility. While there are individual horror stories of illegal aliens kept in a virtual bondage, these appear to be isolated instances. Given the elaborate information network among illegal aliens, especially among the more numerous Mexican illegal aliens, and the considerable degree of geographic mobility, it would be difficult for any employer to consistently pay lower wages than illegal aliens could obtain elsewhere and still recruit and retain illegal alien workers.

The survey data provide some inferential evidence on the exploitation issue. To the extent that exploitation is defined as payment of a wage below the federal minimum wage, it appears to be rare or nonexistent in these data. As discussed above, at a time when the standard federal minimum wage was $3.35 per hour, the average wage for the Mexican illegal aliens in the sample was $4.42 per hour, and for the other illegal aliens $4.73. Only 45 of the 279 aliens (16 percent) who reported their earnings received less than the legal minimum wage. Of these, 18 (of whom 12 were Mexican nationals) were in the restaurant sector where their reported wages may not have included tips and the value of free meals. Because of the "tip-credit," a lower federal minimum wage is applicable for many covered restaurant workers. Another 26 aliens (16 Mexican nationals) were in other services and one alien (not a Mexican national) was in manufacturing. For those in part-time employment who reported a daily or weekly wage, the estimation procedure underestimated their hourly wage. Others may have been in jobs not covered by the federal minimum wage (e.g., local lawn care services).

To the extent that very low wages do exist, they are received only by very recent illegal aliens. The data indicate a sharp rise in wages with duration of residence, with wages showing the sharpest increase in the first few years in the U.S. While to some extent this reflects low-wage recipients either quickly leaving the country or being apprehended early, it may also reflect direct improvements in wage opportunities with duration of residence for the same worker.

Even after controlling for age and country of origin, apprehended illegal aliens in the U.S. a longer period of time are more likely to be working in more skilled, higher-wage sectors of the labor market. This suggests considerable labor market mobility, which would be inconsistent with a widespread practice of exploitation.

There may be some confusion of ethnic enclave employment with exploitation. The degree to which illegal aliens work within an ethnic labor market does not seem to decline with duration of U.S. residence. There is, however, *no* evidence in these data that ethnic enclave employment has an adverse effect on illegal alien wages. Apparently, there is enough mobility in and out of ethnic enclave employment so that wages are equalized for workers of a given skill level.

In a study of the wage rates received in the U.S. by migrants who had returned to Mexico, Kossoudji and Ranney (1984) investigated the effect of legal status. In this sample of 540 men, Kossoudji and

Ranney found that earnings were the same, other measured variables held constant, for legal migrants and for those who entered the U.S. legally but worked in violation of their visa or entry papers and hence were illegal aliens. They also found that both groups earned about 30 percent more than those who entered the U.S. illegally, with the earnings differential varying inversely with the level of skill. This suggests that it is not being an illegal alien worker *per se* that is associated with lower U.S. earnings, but some other unmeasured characteristic associated with entry without inspection. It also suggests the potential sample selection bias inherent in comparative studies of legal and illegal aliens. That is, observed earnings differences may arise from the unmeasured characteristics that determine legal status, rather than from differential opportunities in the U.S.

Douglas Massey (1987) used data on about 300 legal and illegal aliens from four communities in Mexico to study the exploitation issue. Although illegal aliens have significantly lower U.S. wages than the legal aliens, the wage differential disappears when skill and demographic variables are held constant. There was also no effect of legal status, other variables the same, on whether the illegal alien was in an unskilled job. Massey did find, however, that the illegal aliens had a shorter period of employment on their most recent U.S. job. This would result in less investment in training specific to their U.S. employer.

David North and Marion Houstoun asked the nearly 800 apprehended illegal aliens in their 1975 nationwide survey whether they thought that, as a result of their illegal status, they were paid lower wages than legal workers doing the same work. They report that 16 percent felt they were paid lower wages (North and Houstoun, 1976, pp. 132-4). This belief was most common among illegal aliens working in the counties along the Mexican border, and was rare elsewhere. It was also rare among non-Mexican illegal aliens. In addition, they indicate that "illegals who reported exploitation of this kind were almost twice as likely to have been in the

United States less than two years (about half of the sample) than illegals who had been in the United States two or more years."

The greater perception of exploitation along the Mexican border and among recent illegal aliens in the North-Houstoun data may arise from the illegal aliens inappropriately comparing themselves with legal workers who have been in the U.S. for several years, rather than with recent immigrants. Furthermore, illegal aliens in the U.S. for several years, particularly if they are not in the economically depressed border counties, may be more effective in finding jobs in which their skills are most highly rewarded. In addition, given a high degree of voluntary (and due to deportations, involuntary) to-and-from migration among recent illegal aliens along the border, employers may view them as a less stable workforce, and hence a less attractive workforce for employer-financed investments in training. This may result in less training overall and hence in wages that are lower than those received by legal immigrants.

In the Rita Simon and Margo DeLey (1984) survey of legal and illegal alien Mexican women in Los Angeles, the respondents were asked if they felt they had been discriminated against in the U.S. labor market on the basis of their nationality or legal status. In the illegal alien sample, about 20 percent reported discrimination. Nearly half said that their employer knew of their illegal status when they were hired. Interestingly, among those in the control sample of legal aliens, 20 percent also reported discrimination. There was, therefore, no difference in the perception of discrimination between legal and illegal aliens. No other information was provided on the characteristics of the women who reported that they experienced discrimination.

Another perspective is provided by Wayne Cornelius' study of illegal aliens who returned to their home villages in Mexico. Cornelius (1976, p. 27) reports:

> Illegal migrants are not necessarily paid at lower rates than legal workers at their place of employment—indeed, none of the illegals whom we interviewed claimed that they had been discriminated

against in this way. Rather, wages paid for certain types of jobs (particularly in agriculture) were uniformly low, at least by United States standards.[17]

In summary, it appears that concerns over widespread exploitation of illegal aliens are without foundation. The low wages of illegal aliens seems to be a result of their low skill level. They tend to have low levels of schooling and, perhaps because they and their employers perceive their migration as temporary, they have fewer investments in training specific to the U.S. labor market.

V. Summary

This chapter has analyzed the labor market behavior of the sample of nearly 300 male illegal aliens apprehended in the Chicago metropolitan area labor market in 1983. The illegal aliens tend to be young (average age 30.6 years) and to have been in the U.S. a short period of time during their most recent illegal stay (average duration 3.4 years).

The average hourly wage in 1983 of the illegal aliens was $4.52, where Mexican nationals received $4.42 and other nationals received $4.73. Only 16 percent, nearly all in restaurant and other service jobs, reported wage rates below the federal minimum level. Not all of the reported wages below the federal minimum level were in violation of federal law.

The regression analysis of wages showed that there are systematic effects of worker and employer characteristics. The skills of illegal aliens matter; wages are higher the greater the number of years of premigration and postmigration labor market experience, and the greater the number of years working for their current employer. Wages are lower for those who entered under a student visa. Money wages are lower in restaurant jobs, but this may reflect the under-reporting of tip income and the value of free meals.

Part of the rise in wages with the duration of residence in the U.S. or with tenure on the current job is attributable to the characteristics of the employer. Illegal aliens have higher wages if they work for "more desirable" establishments, that is, establishments that are unionized, have a higher wage structure, and have relatively more skilled workers.

The wages of illegal aliens, other things the same, are apparently unrelated to the size of the establishment, whether it is independently owned or a branch/subsidiary, and the proportion of recent immigrants among those hired in the past year, when the firms' wage level and other variables are held constant. The latter implies that the tendency for illegal aliens, particularly those from Mexico, to work with other recent immigrants of the same origin—the ethnic enclave effect—does not tend to depress their wages. The smaller set of job opportunities available to illegal aliens in the ethnic enclave may be offset by the advantages from working in an environment in which country-of-origin skills, particularly language skills, may be more valuable. Opportunities for employment outside the ethnic enclave would eliminate any differences in wages between ethnic enclave and outside jobs.

The characteristics of the employers of illegal aliens vary systematically with the aliens' characteristics. The acquisition of more knowledge and skills relevant for the U.S. labor market with a longer duration of residence increases the likelihood of working for a larger, more highly unionized establishment in manufacturing that has a higher wage structure and a more highly skilled workforce. European and Canadian illegal aliens are more likely to work for these more desirable establishments. Mexican illegal aliens are more likely to be employed in seasonal jobs. This many complement illegal alien preferences for seasonal employment, given the low cost of to-and-fro migration for Mexican nationals. There is evidence of ethnic enclave employment patterns, especially for Mexican illegal aliens, and, in this sample, this tendency does not diminish with duration of residence in the U.S.

These findings indicate that it would be inappropriate to characterize illegal aliens, as is often done, as being locked into low-wage dead-end jobs with flat experience-earnings profiles or as having so little job mobility that they are susceptible to employer exploitation. The data suggest that illegal aliens in the U.S. a longer period of time earn higher wages and work for different types of employers. Job mobility, rather than immobility, may be the best characterization of the U.S. labor market experience of illegal aliens. Perhaps this is not surprising since, in spite of U.S. law, they have engaged in one of the most dramatic types of mobility—international migration. Yet, their wages tend to be low by U.S. standards apparently because of their very low skill levels.

NOTES

[1] There is very little difference in duration in the U.S. and method of entry by country of origin between the subsample for which employer data are available and the subsample whose employers could not be identified or interviewed.

[2] This increases one's confidence that the employer survey data are drawn from a random sample of employers of apprehended illegal aliens, rather than a selected sample.

[3] Country-of-origin regression coefficients comparable to the regressions computed for table 4-5, columns (1) to (3), but without the method of entry variables.[a]

| | | Sample with employer characteristics | |
Country of Origin	Full Sample	Not Held Constant	Held Constant[b]
	(1)	(2)	(3)
EUROCAN	0.2112 (2.619)	0.2503 (2.699)	0.0912 (0.992)
LATAMER	-0.0395 (-0.081)	-0.0327 (-0.620)	-0.0469 (-0.949)
ASIA/AFRI	-0.0684 (-0.886)	0.0420 (0.465)	-0.0105 (-0.122)
Number of Observations	272	184	170

a. Holding constant experience, time in the U.S., and marital status.
b. Also holding constant wages paid high school graduates, degree of unionization, and industry.

[4] The negative coefficient becomes statistically significant when job tenure variables are held constant.

[5] In 3 percent of the 286 cases for which TIMEUS and JOBTENURE can be calculated job tenure is longer than the recent illegal stay. This could arise if an

alien stays on a job longer than is permitted by a temporary work permit, or more likely, if the illegal alien leaves the U.S. and retains his job when he returns. For 14 percent employment with the current employer began within the first month of the current illegal stay.

6 Partial effect of the region variables for Mexican illegal aliens (N = 212).

Partial Effect of Regional Variables	Dependent Variable		
	LINEARN	LNUSER	LNHRPA
WESTCO	-0.35	-0.32	-0.10
	(-2.34)	(-2.19)	(-1.35)
SWBORD	-0.40	-0.52	-0.21
	(-2.88)	(-3.84)	(-3.25)

The larger coefficients for annual earnings may reflect a shorter workweek along the West Coast and the southwestern border.

7 Most of the Mexican illegal aliens in the North-Houstoun data who were not on the West Coast or along the southwestern border were in the Midwest. Hence, the estimated differential reflected Midwest wage opportunities.

8 The union effect is well-established (see for example, Lewis, 1983 or Freeman, 1984). For research on the positive effect of working in a larger firm or establishment on wages, see, for example, Mellow (1982).

9 Data are not available on whether the illegal alien is a member of the union.

10 Mexico (MEXICO) serves as the benchmark. The dichotomous country variables are Europe/Canada (EUROCAN), other Latin America and Caribbean (LATAMER), and Asia, Africa and other areas (ASIA/AFRI).

11 Tests indicated that marital status and legal status at entry generally have no statistically significant effect on the establishment characteristics under study.

12 Barron, Block and Lowenstein (1987) show that larger employers engage in more search in the labor market, offer higher starting wages and provide more on-the-job training.

13 Only 19 percent of the observations were in the U.S. for more than 5 and less than 10 years, and only 5 percent were in the U.S. for 10 or more years.

14 There are no country of origin differences in the tendency to work for a subsidiary or branch (SUBBR) or in a privately owned establishment in contrast to a corporation (PVTOWN).

15 For evidence consistent with a preference for seasonal migration patterns among Mexican illegal aliens, see Cornelius (1976) and Diez-Canedo (1980).

16 Although it has been a violation of federal law to discriminate on the basis of race, ethnicity or national origin since the mid-1960s, discrimination against

aliens *per se* was not illegal. The 1986 Immigration Reform and Control Act, which instituted penalties against employers for knowingly hiring illegal aliens, also makes it illegal for employers to discriminate against aliens who have a legal right to work.

[17] A collaborator of Cornelius confirmed this conclusion, and elaborated that the issue of an illegal status did not matter since if a higher wage were available elsewhere the aliens would quit and take the other job (Diez-Canedo, 1980, p. 96 and 106).

5

The Employers of Illegal Aliens

The public policy interest in illegal aliens appears to focus almost as much on their employers as it does on the aliens themselves. There is a presumption that most illegal aliens come to the U.S. for work. They are drawn to the U.S. by the prospect of high wages and perhaps greater opportunities for job training, relative to what they could receive in their home country. Alternatively, it is argued that U.S. employers use wages and training opportunities as a lure to attract predominantly low-skilled workers to: relieve labor bottlenecks, perform jobs that native workers "will not" perform, or further depress wages or discourage unionization in low-wage, generally nonunion jobs. These alternatives are, of course, the supply and demand sides in the illegal alien labor market.

This public policy focus on employers is unique. There is no similar attention given to other sources of the well-being of illegal aliens, such as the income transfer, educational and social service systems. Nor is there a similar degree of attention devoted to the competition by illegal aliens in consumption. There are no proposals for sanctions against school districts or universities that "knowingly" enroll illegal aliens or against landlords who "knowingly" rent to illegal aliens. Indeed, the Supreme Court has ruled that public school districts cannot discriminate against school-age illegal alien children by denying them access or charging tuition as a condition of enrollment.

In the spirit of the public policy debate, and recognizing the importance of labor market impacts, this study of illegal aliens has focused on the labor market and on the employers of illegal aliens.

It would be futile to try to learn about illegal alien employers merely through a study of illegal aliens. Even if the illegal aliens themselves, rather than their I-213 forms, could have been surveyed, data on many of the most interesting and important characteristics of their employers could not be obtained. Few workers, legal or otherwise, can report on many characteristics of the establishment in which they work including its age, business organization, pay scale, provision of job training, etc. And, even if illegal aliens could provide this information, analyzed in isolation the data would be meaningless. The data can make sense only in a comparative perspective. Hence, for this project, data were collected on employers of illegal aliens and on randomly selected employers.

The establishment survey that is integral to the analysis is unique. There is no comparable systematic survey of employers of illegal aliens, and none that provides linkages with the alien or, for comparative purposes, a parallel sample of randomly selected employers.

As indicated in chapter 3, the establishments interviewed for the employer survey were drawn from two sources. One source was the Record of Deportable Alien, the I-213 form, filed in the Chicago District Office of the Immigration and Naturalization Service in 1983. One data element on the I-213 is the name and address of the current or most recent employer in the U.S. Only establishments in the Chicago SMSA were eligible for the survey. The sample of illegal aliens was stratified by nationality (Mexican and non-Mexican) and by industry (manufacturing, restaurant and other services), but random sampling was used within the six nationality-industry cells. The employers identified from this source are referred to as the INS sample.

The other source of employers were establishments in the Chicago SMSA listed in industry directories for manufacturing and services, and telephone listings in the Yellow Pages for restaurants. Random sampling was used within each industry strata except that the Chicago-Suburban proportions in the INS sample were retained in the general sample. It is not known whether the establishments in the general sample actually employed illegal aliens, knowingly or otherwise. There is, however, a presumption that within major industry categories, randomly selected employers are likely to be less intensive in their employment of illegal aliens than are establishments identified by apprehended illegal aliens as their employers.

This chapter presents the analysis of the differences in the characteristics of the employers selected from the two sources.[1] Because it was not possible to remove illegal alien employers from the general sample, the analysis generates downward biased estimates of differences between the employers of illegal aliens and those who do not hire illegal aliens. An important theme of this chapter will be to try to disentangle the effects on the characteristics of their employers of the temporary or recent migration status of the aliens from their illegal work status. Section I provides descriptive statistics on the response rates and the age and detailed industry of the establishments in the sample. Section II is a regression analysis based on a simple model of the differences between the illegal alien employers and randomly selected employers. Section III focuses on the issue of the "underground economy." In particular, it is concerned with whether the employers of illegal aliens are more likely to pay workers in cash rather than by check and are less likely to require that newly hired workers report their social security number. An analysis of employer differences in the extent of on-the-job training provided by the establishment is in Section IV. Section V considers differences in the understanding of legal liabilities during the hiring process for the two groups of employers. Section VI summarizes the findings in the chapter.

I. Some Descriptive Statistics

There had been a concern that the employers of illegal aliens would avoid any contact with interviewers. If the stereotypical illegal alien employer is a small, "underground" economy (or informal economy) establishment, it would do its best to avoid revealing its existence and hiring practices. Even though at the time of the interview hiring illegal aliens was not illegal, there was reason to believe that many employers thought it was (Chiswick and Fullam, 1980). The expectation was that illegal alien employers would be far more difficult to interview than the general sample employers. Fortunately, this expectation proved to be incorrect.

The full sample includes 406 employers for whom a questionnaire was completed. Of these, 193 were identified by an apprehended illegal alien on the I-213 form and, by coincidence, 213 were from the general sample. The interview completion rate may be defined conservatively as completed interviews as a proportion of establishments not known to be ineligible for the survey. The denominator includes refusals, partial interviews and establishments for which no disposition has been established, as well as completed interviews. The conservative interview completion rate was 76 percent for the INS sample of employers and 79 percent for the general sample. The partial interview rate, that is, the proportion of interviews with more than a minimum amount of item nonresponses, was low in both samples, although it was slightly higher for the employers identified from the INS records. The item nonresponse rate among completed interviews was also low for most questions and there was no systematic pattern on the basis of whether the employer had been identified by an apprehended illegal alien. Thus, illegal alien employers do not appear to be more difficult to interview than randomly selected employers.

It is often said that illegal alien employers are "fly by night" operators. That is, that they are relatively new businesses, at the margin of profitability, with a high failure rate. If not for labor that is "cheap" because of the workers' illegal status, they could not stay in business. It was not possible to obtain data on profit rates, but it was possible to address the issue of the "age" of the establishment.

The respondents were asked to report the number of years the establishment has been in operation. There appears to be no difference in the distribution of age of establishment between the INS illegal alien sample and the general sample.[2] About 2 percent of the establishments in the INS sample and 3 percent of the establishments in the general sample were relatively young—they had been in business less than two years. About one-quarter of the establishments in each sample had been in operation for at least two and up to ten years, and nearly three-quarters in each sample had been in business ten or more years.

As a result of the sampling procedures, however, the INS sample of employers consists of large establishments, and larger establishments tend to have been in business longer. Controlling for the size of the establishment, there is a nonlinear effect of its age on the probability the establishment is on the INS sample.[3] Among the youngest establishments the probability that it is in the INS sample rises with age, although at a decreasing rate, until a peak at 4.7 years. Beyond 4.7 years the probability decreases with age. This pattern is not consistent with the "fly by night" establishment hypothesis, even though illegal alien employers are less numerous among older firms when establishment size is held constant.

An analysis of the distribution of illegal alien employers by industry is limited by the stratification procedures employed in the survey. Because of the predominance of restaurants in illegal alien employment and greater homogeneity in this sector, stratified sampling was used with target numbers of cases for each of three broad industries: manufacturing, restaurants, and other services. Within these broad sectors (and two nationality categories in the INS sample) employers were randomly selected.

The specific product or service of the establishment was recorded and each establishment was coded by industry. The manufacturing category includes durable and nondurable manufacturing as well as construction. Within the manufacturing category, construction firms are about 16 percent (15 establishments) of the general sample but only 4 percent (3 establishments) of the INS sample. Among manufacturing establishments, almost two-thirds were in durable goods and about one-third were in nondurable goods in each of the two samples.[4] The highly unionized nature of the construction industry in the Chicago SMSA may be responsible for the small proportion of construction establishments in the INS sample.

There are some differences in the distribution by specific industry in the other (nonrestaurant) services category, although the sample sizes are too small to do separate analyses by subsector.[5] In the INS sample of 62 service sector establishments, landscaping is the most common service, comprising over one-quarter of the establishments and nearly half of the establishments identified by a Mexican illegal alien. Retail trade is the next most common industry with just under one-quarter of the establishments. For non-Mexican illegal aliens, who appear to have a higher level of skill, the health sector and transportation and utilities rivaled retail trade. In the general sample, retail trade was the most common service industry with nearly two-fifths of the establishments, and, in spite of a deliberate oversampling to try to have greater comparability with the INS sample, landscaping consisted of about one-twentieth of the general sample. Business and repair services along with finance, insurance, and real estate were each about one-fifth of the establishments.

Clearly, in the nonrestaurant service sector, landscaping firms are a major source of employment for Mexican illegal aliens and a prime target of INS enforcement activities. In the Chicago area, with a long, cold winter, landscaping is an ideal type of employment for low-skilled workers from farm or rural backgrounds seeking seasonal employment. The landscapers work in monolingual (Spanish) crews and many workers may return to the same employer year after year.

The non-Mexican illegal aliens in other services have a sectorial distribution close to that in the general sample. However, they appear to be somewhat more concentrated in the health and transportation and utilities sectors, and less so in finance, insurance and real estate (FIRE). The underrepresentation of illegal aliens in the FIRE sector may arise from fewer opportunities for the employment of less-skilled, non-English speaking workers and the licensing requirements for some jobs (e.g., real estate agents).

In summary, the data suggest considerable similarity between establishments in the INS and general samples. They were equally cooperative in granting and completing the interview and have about the same age distribution. Illegal aliens appear to be widely dispersed among the industries in the Chicago area economy. Mexican illegal aliens are more intensive in the restaurant and landscaping sectors. Jobs in these sectors are well-suited to low-skilled workers with rural backgrounds who view themselves, or are viewed by their employers, as temporary migrants and therefore do not make large investments in job training specific to the U.S., and have a preference for jobs with seasonal employment. Illegal aliens in general, but especially Mexican illegal aliens, tend to be under-represented in the finance, insurance and real estate industries. Jobs in these sectors are more likely to be white collar, and hence require a higher level of skill, including facility in English.

II. Differences Between Illegal Alien Employers and Other Employers

This section is concerned with developing and testing hypotheses that may differentiate employers of illegal aliens from randomly selected employers. The dependent variable is the dichotomous variable ILLEMP, which is unity if the establishment was identified by an apprehended illegal alien (INS sample) and is zero if it was selected from the general population of employers. This is actually an oversimplification of the concept of employment of illegal aliens which is necessitated by the data. The number of employers in the general sample who also employ illegal aliens is not known. In addition, among those who do employ illegal aliens, regardless of the sample, there are no data on the number or the share of illegal aliens in the workforce, whether they are temporary or permanent workers, or their occupations. It is assumed, however, that the intensity of illegal alien employment is greater in the INS sample.

As was shown in chapter 4, apprehended illegal aliens employed in the Chicago metropolitan area are disproportionately, low-skilled recent migrants from non-English speaking countries with presumably limited information about the U.S. labor market. Many view their stay in the U.S. as temporary and hence they have less incentive than permanent settlers to invest in skills specific to the U.S. labor market. This encourages ethnic enclave employment, which provides a sheltered environment for those not making U.S.-specific investments and a transition work environment for other illegal alien workers.

Employment in an ethnic enclave is also encouraged by the nontrivial expected cost of being deported and then returning to the U.S. Although the probability that an illegal alien who has success-fully penetrated the border will be "detected" (arrested) in the interior is low, it is greater than zero and a constant concern of illegal aliens. The cost to the illegal alien of an apprehension, deportation and return to the U.S. is also relatively low for a Mexican national, but it is higher for other illegal aliens. The incentive to avoid detection encourages employment in areas where they, or their illegal status, will be less visible to the immigration enforcement authorities. This would also encourage ethnic enclave employment if there is a large group of legal resident aliens and U.S. citizens of the same national origin with whom the illegal aliens can "blend."

The temporary nature of much illegal migration and the incen-tives to leave dependent family members in the country of origin also affect seasonality of employment. Illegal aliens have an incen-tive to prefer jobs in which there is little penalty for interrupted employment during long visits outside the U.S. While jobs with little firm-specific or U.S.-specific training partially satisfy this condition, more preferable would be seasonal jobs in which wage rates and employment are greater in the "on season" and, by definition, much lower in the "off season." Because of the lower costs of return or cyclical migration, the Mexican illegal aliens would exhibit a greater labor supply for seasonal jobs than other illegal aliens.

Illegal alien employers are believed to have a low degree of unionization. It is often alleged that one purpose of hiring illegal aliens is to thwart unionization efforts. Furthermore, to the extent that unions raise wage rates, establishments have an incentive to employ higher-skilled workers so as to reduce, if not close, the gap between the union wage and worker productivity. In addition, higher-skilled native workers may be more readily available at the union wage. Finally, native workers may use the unionization of their establishment as a mechanism for reducing competition from illegal alien workers by excluding them from the hiring process.

The media and popular literature also portray illegal aliens as working for smaller, more informal business establishments in which the decisionmaker is the owner rather than for establishments that are part of a larger enterprise. These smaller, private establishments are more likely to have informal hiring requirements and hence would be less concerned with the legal status of their workers.

These considerations, some of which refer primarily to temporary workers and others primarily to the illegal status of the workers, suggest several testable hypotheses. It is hypothesized that illegal alien employers (ILLEMP) are less unionized (UNION), less likely to be a branch or subsidiary of a larger firm (SUBBR), and maintain a seasonal pattern to employment (SEASONAL). The ethnic enclave hypothesis suggests that the owners are more likely to be Hispanic (HISPOWN) and the co-workers of Hispanic or Asian origin (MINORRACE).[6] Table 5-1 presents an explanation of the variables and their codes.[7]

Because of missing observations, the regression analysis of the differences between the INS sample and the general sample has 399 observations, 7 less than the full sample. The sample used for the comparison of establishments includes 189 illegal alien employers and 210 employers from the general sample. The means and standard deviations of the variables are reported in table 5-2. The employers identified by an illegal alien are, on average, three times the size of the general sample of employers, and this may well be the result of the sampling methodology. Some of the other explanatory variables, however, vary with establishment size, such as degree of unionization and whether the establishment is a branch/subsidiary or is independently owned. Thus, the greater degree of unionization

Table 5-1
Variable List

Code	Description
Dependent Variable	
ILLEMP	Employer identified by an apprehended illegal alien = 1; otherwise = 0.
Independent Variables	
SIZE, SIZESQ	Total number of employees, and its square.
UNION	Percentage of nonsupervisory employees who are union members.
MANUF, REST, SERVICE	Industry of establishment: manufacturing and construction; restaurant; other service.
SUBBR	Type of ownership subsidiary or branch = 1; otherwise = 0.
SEASONAL	Dummy for existence of patterns of seasonal employment = 1; otherwise = 0.
HISPOWN	Dummy for Hispanic ownership = 1; otherwise = 0.
MINORRACE	Percentage of employees who are of Hispanic or Asian origin.

and the greater frequency of branch and subsidiary establishments in the illegal alien employer sample may not reflect a partial effect (i.e., controlling for establishment size) but rather the larger size.

The multivariate regression analyses of the dichotomous variable ILLEMP, are reported in tables 5-3 and 5-4 using ordinary least squares (OLS) procedures and in table 5-5 using logit analysis. Tables 5-3 and 5-4 differ merely by the inclusion of the variable for the ethnic composition of the workforce (MINORRACE) in the former. This variable is potentially endogenous. An establishment is more likely to have a larger proportion of minority workers if it was identified by a minority worker. There is virtually no difference in the interpretations derived from these two tables. The OLS analysis is to be preferred over the logit analysis for its simplicity of presentation and interpretation, but the standard errors are biased by heteroskedastic residuals. The logit analysis corrects for the bias

Table 5-2
Means and Standard Deviations of Variables
by Type of Employer

Variable	INS sample (1)	General sample (2)	Total sample (3)
SIZE	155.063 (305.104)	51.557 (194.074)	100.586 (257.736)
UNION (%)	29.306 (42.722)	20.271 (36.584)	24.550 (39.816)
MANUF	0.370 (0.484)	0.452 (0.499)	0.414 (0.493)
REST	0.302 (0.460)	0.186 (0.390)	0.241 (0.428)
SERVICE	0.328 (0.471)	0.362 (0.482)	0.346 (0.476)
SUBBR	0.275 (0.448)	0.224 (0.418)	0.248 (0.432)
SEASONAL	0.471 (0.500)	0.314 (0.465)	0.388 (0.488)
HISPOWN	0.037 (0.189)	0.019 (0.137)	0.028 (0.164)
MINNORRACE (%)	44.854 (28.797)	18.051 (23.002)	30.747 (29.139)
SAMPLE SIZE	189	210	399

in the standard errors. In general, the two procedures give the same results in this study.[8] Column (1) in tables 5-3, 5-4 and 5-5 is for all industries, columns (2) to (4) are separate analyses by industry. A Chow-test for the OLS regressions indicates that the structures of the equations differ significantly across the three industries (table 5-3 equations, observed F-statistic $F = 10.3$).

Table 5-3
Regression Analysis of Characteristics of Employers—Ordinary Least Squares Analyses Controlling for the Racial Composition of Employees[a]
(Dependent Variable: Employer Selected From INS Sample)

Variable	All employers (1)	Manuf. & construction (2)	Restaurant (3)	Other service (4)
SIZE	0.00134	0.00177	0.00608	0.00085
	(6.629)	(5.461)	(2.752)	(3.162)
SIZESQ[b]	-5.277	-7.224	-8.402	-3.413
	(-5.229)	(-3.546)	(-2.502)	(-2.830)
UNION	0.00130	0.00122	-1.40987	0.00241
	(2.276)	(1.662)	(-0.499)	(2.649)
SUBBR	-0.041	-0.067	-0.219	0.115
	(-0.830)	(-0.911)	(-2.068)	(-1.455)
SEASONAL	0.112	0.025	-0.005	0.285
	(2.665)	(0.369)	(-0.053)	(4.265)
HISPOWN	-0.141	0.542	-0.521	-0.119
	(-1.084)	(2.289)	(-2.530)	(-0.447)
MINORRACE	0.00789	0.00601	0.01077	0.00888
	(10.699)	(5.560)	(6.163)	(7.618)
MANUF	-0.326	n.a.	n.a.	n.a.
	(-5.748)			
SERVICE	-0.179	n.a.	n.a.	n.a.
	(-3.239)			
Constant	0.272	0.007	0.175	-0.021
	(5.309)	(0.111)	(1.914)	(-0.390)
Adjusted R^2	0.352	0.356	0.318	0.482
Number of observations	399	165	96	138

a. A Chow test of the null hypothesis of identical structures across the three industry types is rejected. The calculated F-value is 10.28, the critical value is $F(8,363; .01) = 2.55$.

b. Regression coefficient = stated coefficient x 10^{-7}.

n.a. = variable not entered in the equation.

t-ratios are in parentheses.

Table 5-4

Regression Analysis of Characteristics of Employers—Ordinary Least Squares Analyses
(Dependent Variable: Employer Selected from INS Sample)

Variable	All employers (1)	Manuf. & construction (2)	Restaurant (3)	Other service (4)
SIZE	-0.2016	0.0021	0.0081	0.0012
	(-3.215)	(5.965)	(3.046)	(3.796)
SIZESQ[a]	-6.800	-9.2569	-0.0010	-5.0813
	(-6.007)	(-4.243)	(-2.594)	(-3.562)
UNION	0.0013	0.0012	-0.0004	0.0028
	(2.040)	(1.513)	(-0.113)	(2.646)
SUBBR	-0.0911	-0.0866	-0.1935	-0.0104
	(-1.531)	(-1.041)	(-1.352)	(-0.105)
SEASONAL	0.1526	0.0403	-0.0638	0.4092
	(3.212)	(0.547)	(-0.612)	(5.251)
HISPOWN	0.2257	0.7362	0.0765	0.3510
	(1.595)	(2.886)	(0.359)	(1.131)
MINORRACE	n.a.	n.a.	n.a.	n.a.
MANUF	-0.2564	n.a.	n.a.	n.a.
	(-4.026)			
SERVICE	-0.2016	n.a.	n.a.	n.a.
	(-3.215)			
Constant	0.4577	0.2005	0.3967	0.1412
	(8.404)	(3.615)	(4.040)	(2.386)
Adjusted R^2	0.167	0.235	0.048	0.254
Number of observations	399	165	96	138

a. Regression coefficient = stated coefficient x 10^{-7}.

n.a. = variable not entered in regression.

t-statistics in parentheses.

Table 5-5

**Logit Analysis of Characteristics of
Employers—Maximum Likelihood Estimation
(Dependent Variable: Employer Selected From INS Sample)**

Variable	All employers (1)	Manuf. & construction (2)	Restaurant (3)	Other service (4)
SIZE	0.0106 (5.036)	0.0122 (2.632)	0.0105 (0.217)	0.0068 (2.334)
SIZESQ[a]	-4.148 (-3.811)	-3.615 (-0.361)	227.225 (0.395)	-2.636 (-2.092)
UNION	0.0077 (2.079)	0.0068 (1.433)	-0.0177 (-1.009)	0.0146 (2.134)
SUBBR	-0.296 (-0.916)	-0.504 (-0.989)	-1.758 (-2.136)	1.027 (1.635)
SEASONAL	0.657 (2.470)	0.135 (3.065)	-0.104 (-0.175)	2.026 (3.567)
HISPOWN	-0.852 (-0.986)	21.065 (0.002)	-7.622 (-3.140)	-0.680 (-0.332)
MINORRACE	0.0456 (8.055)	0.0342 (4.325)	0.1137 (4.487)	0.0579 (4.990)
MANUF	-2.047 (-5.429)	n.a.	n.a.	n.a.
SERVICE	-0.999 (-2.970)	n.a.	n.a.	n.a.
Constant	-1.356 (-4.400)	-2.850 (-5.702)	-2.201 (-2.379)	-3.497 (-5.764)
Number of observations	399	165	96	138

a. Actual coefficient = stated coefficient x 10^{-6}.

n.a. = variable not entered in the equation.

t-ratios are in parentheses.

In these data, the illegal alien employers are larger, that is, they have more employees (SIZE), than the general sample employers, even when other variables are the same. The probability that the employer was drawn from the illegal alien sample rises with the number of employees in each industry in the range of the data. To some extent this may reflect a substitution of a larger number of lower-skilled illegal alien workers for capital (both physical capital and skills per worker), other things the same. It is, however, also consistent with the bias in establishment size generated by the sampling methodology. At this stage it is not possible to separate the effects of these competing hypotheses.

Controlling for establishment size, the greater the degree of unionization (UNION), the higher the probability that the establishment was identified by an apprehended illegal alien.[9] This effect is significant in the all industries (pooled) analysis and for nonrestaurant services. Tests for nonlinearities in the effect of unionization did not result in additional statistically significant findings.

Restaurants that are independently owned, as distinct from a branch or subsidiary of a larger firm, are more likely to be employers of illegal aliens, but only when the racial/ethnic composition of the workforce is held constant.[10] Otherwise there is no effect of type of ownership on whether the establishment is in the INS sample.

There is a tendency for the employers of illegal aliens to be more likely to report seasonal patterns (SEASONAL) in their employment. For the sample pooled across industries, in other services, and in the logit analysis for manufacturing, the employers indicating seasonality were more likely to be from the illegal alien sample. There is no significant difference in seasonality reported for the restaurant sector. As one would expect, the "off season" is most intense in the winter (December to February). A distinguishing feature between the two samples of employers, however, is the greater incidence of the fall (September to November) being part of the "off season" for the illegal alien employers.[11] This does not reflect the greater incidence of lawn care services in the illegal alien sample. When a dichotomous control variable for lawn care service is included in the equation, the slope coefficient of the seasonal variable is reduced, but it is still large and highly significant.

In summary, the employers in the INS sample in manufacturing and other services are more likely to report seasonality in employment, and if they do, the off season is longer than in the general sample. It should be remembered though that workers may, by choice have a seasonal pattern in their employment, even if there is no seasonality for the establishment.

Although there are very few Hispanic owners, this variable appears to be significant in manufacturing.[12] Among manufacturing establishments in the OLS analysis, Hispanic owners are more likely to be in the INS sample. The significant Hispanic owner coefficient with an unexpected sign in the restaurant sample in table 5-3 disappears when the ethnic composition of the workers is deleted in table 5-4.

The extent to which Hispanics and Asians are represented in the establishment's workforce (MINORRACE) is an important variable in the analysis. In each of the industrial sectors, the illegal alien employers are characterized by having a larger proportion of employees who are Hispanic or Asian, even after controlling for Hispanic ownership of the establishment. This may reflect the greater probability of an employer being included in the illegal alien sample the greater the number of illegal aliens.[13] The finding is also consistent with an ethnic enclave hypothesis. Illegal aliens, who are predominantly of Hispanic or Asian origin, are more likely to work in establishments with relatively more Hispanics and Asians, other things the same. This interpretation is consistent with the finding for manufacturing that Hispanic owners are more likely to be in the illegal alien sample.

In summary, the employers of illegal aliens have characteristics attractive to temporary or new foreign workers—they are more likely to have seasonality in employment and be part of an ethnic enclave. They are also more highly unionized in the nonrestaurant services sector, but not elsewhere. Type of ownership does not appear to matter.

III. The Underground Economy

A major concern regarding the employers of illegal aliens is whether they operate in the "underground economy." Establishments in the underground economy are not necessarily producing illegal goods or services, but rather they organize their activities, including recordkeeping, so as to illegally avoid the payment of taxes by the firm or its workers, or to illegally avoid compliance with health, safety and labor legislation.[14]

Illegal aliens and underground-economy employers would tend to have an affinity for each other (Simon and Witte, 1982, especially chapter 3). Illegal aliens wish to avoid detection by the authorities. Many lack valid social security numbers, others have fraudulently obtained access to valid social security numbers. Even if they and their employers make contributions to social insurance programs, (e.g., social security, unemployment compensation, and workers' compensation), the illegal aliens may be too fearful to apply for benefits, or may be denied the benefits even if they do apply. As low-skilled and non-English speaking new entrants to the U.S. labor market, their productivity may be so low that the sacrifice of health and safety conditions may be viewed by them as a small price to pay for getting a job which may offer low wages by U.S. standards, but high wages compared to their alternatives in the country of origin.

Employers could not be asked directly if they are part of the underground economy. First, there is no hard and fast distinction between these employers and other or "above-ground" employers. Rather, one may think in terms of varying degrees of subterranean activities; probably no two employers not in full compliance are alike in their behavior. Second, positive responses to direct questions on recordkeeping, payment of taxes, income tax withholding, etc., would necessarily be suspect. However, the survey included two questions that can be used to gauge the extent of participation in the underground economy. One is whether workers were paid in cash or by check. The other is the extent to which workers hired in the past year were required to have a social security number. The emphasis is on actual hiring practice rather than on stated hiring procedures because an earlier survey (Chiswick and Fullam, 1980) revealed considerable disparity between the two.

A characteristic of the underground economy is a preference for transactions in cash rather than by check, as the latter leaves a paper trail. While there is no one-to-one correspondence between payment of workers in cash and participation in the underground economy, there is a presumption that those who do pay by cash are more likely to be eschewing proper recordkeeping and payment of required taxes. Thus, the payment of wages in cash (in part or in total) for workers in the most common male nonsupervisory job may serve as a proxy for being part of the underground economy. There are, of course, two deficiencies with this proxy. First, the method of payment for illegal aliens may differ from the payment method for the most common male nonsupervisory job. Cash payment may be more common for the former than the latter. Second, by limiting the sample to establishments with five or more employees, the study excludes very small establishments and household employers, perhaps the types of employers most likely to pay workers in cash.

Of the 402 employers responding to the question on method of payment, only 3.2 percent (13 employers) reported paying part or all of the wages in cash rather than entirely by check or its modern equivalent, electronic transfer of funds.[15] In the INS sample, 3.6 percent of the establishments reported payment in cash in contrast to the 2.9 percent in the general sample. The difference is very small and not statistically significant. Most of the employers paying in cash were in the restaurant sector (11 of the 13) where the practice was most common among the smaller restaurants.

Thus, acknowledging payment of wages in cash for the most common male nonsupervisory job appears to be rare in manufacturing and service jobs, but not uncommon (about 12 percent) in the restaurant sector. There does not appear to be a difference in this practice between the employers identified by the illegal aliens and randomly selected employers.

Another index of participation in the underground economy is whether the employer required workers hired in the past year to have a social security number. The question on the proportion of hires required to have a social security number was included in a list of actual hiring requirements. All of the establishments in the sample were covered by the social security program and a social security number is used as the taxpayer identification number for the federal and state income tax. Thus, full compliance with the federal and state tax law would require obtaining the social security number of each person hired.

Of the 375 employers who hired workers in the past year and responded to the question, only 10 (2.7 percent) reported that they required social security numbers from less than 100 percent of the workers hired.[16] Among those who were not in full compliance, 40 percent did not require it for any of their hires. The proportion of establishments not requiring the number for all new hires was 3.3 percent for the INS sample and 2.1 percent for the general sample of employers, and the difference is not statistically significant. Although the sample sizes become small, it appears that lack of full compliance is more common among the illegal alien employers in manufacturing (4 out of 71 employers or 6.0 percent) than in the other sectors.

In summary, the two proxy measures for participation in the underground economy, paying workers in cash and not requiring all newly hired workers to provide a social security number, suggest that few employers of five or more workers engage in these practices. Although illegal alien employers may participate somewhat more in the underground economy than randomly selected employers, the differences are very small and are not statistically significant. The most striking pattern is the greater frequency of payment of part or all of wages in cash in both samples in the restaurant sector (about 12 percent of the establishments). This is a sector in which receipts are often primarily or entirely in cash and where monitoring of sales by the tax authorities would be difficult.

IV. On-the-Job Training

The extent to which illegal aliens receive on-the-job training in the U.S. is important for their labor market adjustment, that is, the progress of their earnings, employment and occupational status with duration of residence. It is also important for analyzing their permanence in or degree of attachment to the U.S. labor market. The greater the extent of their investment in training specific to their U.S. employer, their U.S. industry or the U.S. economy, as distinct from perfectly internationally transferable training, the smaller the likelihood of their returning to their country of origin.

Illegal aliens have a smaller incentive, compared to legal immigrants and natives, for making investments in skills that have U.S. specificity. Skills specific to the U.S. are, by definition, of lesser value in the country of origin. Thus, to the extent that illegal aliens view themselves as only temporary migrants, these investments would be less attractive. Even if the illegal aliens would like to plan a permanent residency in the U.S., there is always the possibility of apprehension and deportation. In addition, even if the deported illegal alien subsequently returns, the particular job may no longer be available. To reduce the probability and cost of deportation, many illegal aliens leave dependent family members in the home country and may return home for lengthy visits (see, for example, Cornelius, 1976 and Diez-Canedo, 1980). Skills specific to the U.S. tend to depreciate during a return visit lasting several months and a new job may have to be found after returning to the U.S.

For similar reasons, employers of illegal aliens would be more reluctant to finance part of the firm-specific component of on-the-job training of illegal aliens. Concerns regarding voluntary return visits and deportation add to the degree of uncertainty as to whether an illegal alien in whose skills the establishment has made investments will remain with the firm long enough for the investment to be profitable.

As a result of these employee and employer incentives, it is hypothesized that illegal aliens are likely to have fewer skills acquired on the job that are specific to the U.S. Although the earnings of illegal aliens were analyzed in chapter 4, earnings reflect general as well as specific job skills, and include the skills and knowledge acquired merely by living in an area. There are no direct data on the I-213 or in the employer survey on the extent of on-the-job training received by (or invested in) the illegal aliens. The survey does include information on the number of business days of training in the establishment that a newly-hired worker generally requires to learn to do well the most common male nonsupervisory job. The question was asked for workers with no prior experience in the job and for those with prior experience, without being more specific about the nature or duration of the prior experience. These data can be used to test for differences in the degree of on-the-job training.

The statistical test is performed by regressing the variable ILLEMP on the days of training reported by the establishment, controlling for the total number of employees. The control for establishment size is important, as the extent of on-the-job training rises with the size of the establishment (Barron, Block, and Lowenstein, 1987). Larger firms or establishments are more likely to be able to internalize the benefits from firm-specific training because of greater opportunities for job mobility within the firm and lower quit rates.

There are also systematic differences in the skill level of the most common male nonsupervisory job; the occupational level is substantially lower in the INS sample than in the general sample (table 5-6). Among the manufacturing establishments, only 15.1 percent

Table 5-6

Cross-Tabulation of Most Common Male Nonsupervisory
Job by Type of Employer and by Industry

Occupation	All industries INS sample	All industries General sample	Manufacturing INS sample	Manufacturing General sample	Restaurant INS sample	Restaurant General sample	Other service INS sample	Other service General sample
Managerial/ professional	3 (1.6)	3 (1.4)	1 (1.4)	0 (0.0)	0 (0.0)	0 (0.0)	2 (3.2)	3 (4.1)
Technical	5 (2.6)	46 (21.9)	1 (1.4)	12 (12.5)	0 (0.0)	0 (0.0)	4 (6.5)	34 (45.9)
Production (skilled)	13 (6.8)	29 (13.8)	9 (12.3)	18 (18.8)	0 (0.0)	0 (0.0)	4 (6.5)	11 (14.9)
Service	80 (41.7)	48 (22.9)	2 (2.7)	1 (1.0)	57 (100.0)	39 97.5	21 (33.9)	8 (10.8)
Operator	37 (19.3)	58 (27.6)	32 (43.8)	45 (46.9)	0 (0.0)	1 (2.5)	5 (8.1)	12 (16.2)
Handler	46 (24.0)	24 (11.4)	28 (38.4)	20 (20.8)	0 (0.0)	0 (0.0)	18 (29.0)	4 (5.4)
Agriculture	8 (4.2)	2 (1.0)	0 (0.0)	0 (0.0)	0 (0.0)	0 (0.0)	8 (12.9)	2 (2.7)
Total	192 (100.0)	210 (100.0)	73 (100.0)	96 (100.0)	57 (100.0)	40.0 (100.0)	62 (100.0)	74 (100.0)

NOTES: Entries in the table are cell counts with the cell value as a percent of the column total in parentheses.

of the illegal alien employers in contrast to 31.3 percent of the general sample employers reported that this job was in the professional, technical or skilled production worker category. Among the establishments in the service sector (excluding restaurants), the proportions were 16.2 percent and 64.9 percent, respectively. More highly skilled jobs generally require a longer period of firm-specific training.

There is a very large difference between the average number of days of training to learn to do the job well for workers with and without prior experience in the job. For workers with no prior experience the training is both general and firm-specific, and the mean is 156 days. For workers with prior experience, the training is presumably predominantly firm-specific, and the number of days of training is only 45. Given employee and employer aversion to firm-specific training for illegal aliens, it is to be expected that illegal aliens will work in establishments with jobs that require fewer days of specific training.

Controlling only for the size of the establishment, jobs that require a longer training period are significantly less likely to be in the INS sample.[17] This is not merely a consequence of the occupational mix of the most common male nonsupervisory job. When dichotomous variables are used to control statistically for the seven major occupational categories, the regression coefficients on days of training remain negative. Although the coefficients are smaller, the effect is still statistically significant for workers with prior experience.

Thus, the data are consistent with the hypothesis that male illegal aliens work for employers who provide less on-the-job training.

V. Perceptions of Legal Hiring Requirements

The respondent was the person in charge of hiring for the most common male nonsupervisory job. The survey included a series of questions about the respondent's understanding of the legal liabilities regarding the hiring of illegal aliens. The stub in table 5-7 repeats the 11 questions in the order in which they were asked. Of the 11 questions, 2 referred to the age of the worker to be hired, 2 referred to females, 1 referred to the handicapped, 2 referred to union membership, 1 referred to aliens, and 3 referred to illegal aliens. The nonimmigrant questions served two functions: to provide a benchmark for interpreting responses, and to mask the study's interest in illegal aliens. The columns in table 5-7 indicate the percent of respondents who reported "Yes, Currently the Law" for each of three categories of employers, that is, the general sample and the INS sample by whether the identifying alien was a Mexican national.

Most of the establishments reported that they believed it was not legal to "refuse to hire" older workers, the handicapped, pregnant women, women in strenuous jobs, and union members. The term "refuse to hire" may have encouraged the negative responses. A smaller proportion, but still a majority of respondents reported that they believed they could not legally refuse to hire a person who is not a U.S. citizen. At the time, however, it was legal to discriminate on the basis of alienage.[18]

About two-thirds of the illegal alien employers reported that they thought they were required to check the visa of noncitizen job applicants. Nearly 9 out of 10 employers in the general sample gave this response. In fact, there was no legal requirement at the time of the survey to check or verify the legal status of new hires. These high rates are not simply a response to a question on requirements "to check," as the affirmative responses on checking the age of job applicants are much lower. Only 20 to 25 percent of illegal alien employers reported that an employer may knowingly hire an illegal alien, in contrast to 15 percent in the general sample. For "harboring" (providing a residence and a job) the responses were under 20 percent and 10 percent, respectively.[19]

Thus, most employers believed it was *not* legal to refuse to hire aliens; however, they believed there was an affirmative requirement to check an alien's visa for legal status and that it was not legal

Table 5-7

Percent Responding "Yes, Currently the Law" to Questions on Understanding of Hiring Regulations[a]

	INS sample		General sample	Total
	Mexican alien	Non-Mexican alien		
1. Legally, employers are supposed to check the age of each person they hire. (N=395)	31.9	49.2	42.3	42.5
2. Employers may legally refuse to hire a person over age 65 because of his or her age. (N=376)	12.9	12.1	18.0	15.4
3. Employers may legally refuse to hire a person because he or she is not a U.S. citizen. (N=372)	32.5	20.6	42.6	35.5
4. Legally, if an applicant is not a U.S. citizen, employers are supposed to check to see if he or she has a visa permitting him or her to work in the U.S. (N=388)	63.8	69.6	87.2	77.1
5. Employers may legally refuse to hire a woman because she is pregnant. (N=368)	18.3	16.2	18.3	17.9
6. Legally, employers can require that an applicant be a union member before he or she can be hired. (N=363)	15.2	6.0	23.9	17.9
7. Employers may legally refuse to hire a person because he or she is a union member. (N=375)	1.8	3.1	7.7	5.1
8. Legally, employers may knowingly hire an immigrant who does not have a visa permitting him or her to work. (N=367)	26.4	21.7	15.1	19.6
9. Employers may legally provide a residence, as well as a job, for an immigrant without a visa permitting him or her to work. (N=388)	19.2	19.4	6.8	12.7
10. Employers may legally refuse to hire a person because he or she is handicapped, even if the handicap does not affect the person's productivity. (N=394)	4.2	5.7	9.7	7.4
11. Legally, employers may refuse to hire a woman for a strenuous job because it might injure her health. (N=366)	20.9	36.1	33.0	31.7

a. Responses were "Yes, currently the law," "No, not currently the law," and "Don't know." The maximum potential sample size for each question is 406. Sample sizes (N) and percents exclude "Don't Know" responses and blanks.

knowingly to hire illegal aliens. The general sample employers were more averse to aliens—they were more likely to believe they could refuse to hire aliens, were more likely to believe they were required to check an alien's legal status, and less likely to believe they could legally hire illegal aliens.[20] In the INS sample, differences in responses between employers identified by a Mexican national and other illegal alien employers are generally smaller and show no consistent pattern.

Assuming these responses are truthful, they do not offer much encouragement for the "announcement effect" of the employer sanctions introduced by the Immigration Reform and Control Act of 1986. The 1984 survey indicates that most employers, even in the INS sample, were already under the impression that they were required to check an alien's legal status and that it was against the law to hire illegal aliens. Thus, they believed that employer sanctions were already the law of the land. While this perception may have inhibited the employment opportunities of illegal aliens, as suggested by the difference between the INS sample and the general sample, it did not close them. Presumably the respondents violating what they believed to be legal prohibitions against hiring illegal aliens perceived the probability of detection and the penalties if detected to be sufficiently small or nonexistent.

VI. Summary

The analysis in this chapter indicates areas of similarity and differences between the sample of establishments identified by an apprehended illegal alien and the establishments randomly selected from industry directories. It was not possible to remove from the general sample establishments that employ illegal aliens. As a result, the methodology biases downward differences between employers of illegal aliens and those who do not employ illegal aliens.

There was little systematic difference in the willingness of the two types of establishments to participate in the survey, or in their willingness to respond to particular questions.

The illegal alien employer characteristics are consistent with a model that emphasizes the temporary and relatively recent migration of the aliens. Their employers are more likely than the general sample of employers to exhibit seasonal employment patterns in nonrestaurant services, particularly a longer "off season" in the fall. They are more likely to be part of an ethnic-enclave economy—their employers in manufacturing are more likely to be Hispanic and a greater proportion of their workers are Hispanic or of Asian origin. Apprehended illegal aliens are more heavily concentrated in the restaurant and lawn care industries and apparently are least represented in sectors requiring higher levels of skill, especially skills specific to the U.S. such as fluency in English.

The two samples of establishments differed in the extent to which they provided on-the-job training. The illegal alien employers provided significantly fewer days of training, and the difference between the INS and general sample establishments is larger for firm-specific training than for all on-the-job training. The difference in the amount of training in the two samples was smaller, but still substantial, when the skill level of the workforce was held constant. The skill level of the workers is considerably lower in the establishments known to have employed an illegal alien.

The illegal nature of the presence of the aliens in the U.S. labor market does not appear to be an important direct determinant of their employment patterns; they are not more likely to work in newer or "fly-by-night" establishments, they are not more likely to work for independently owned establishments, and they are not more likely to work in the underground economy, to the extent this can be measured. For example, the payment of workers in part or entirely in cash appears to be the same in the INS and the general sample. Payment in cash is now rare in all sectors, except for small restaurants.

Most establishments believed it was illegal to hire an illegal alien and that they were required to check the visa status of noncitizen job applicants. These perceptions of the law were somewhat stronger in the general sample than in the INS sample, yet both perceptions were incorrect at the time of the survey. These perceptions, which might be viewed as an "announcement effect" of employer sanctions, apparently did not play a major role in reducing job opportunities for illegal aliens. This is a further indication that their illegal status *per se* did not detract from the job opportunities of the illegal aliens. It also suggests that the mere introduction of employer sanctions may not have a significant deterrent effect. For the sanctions to have an impact may require substantial resources devoted to enforcement and substantial penalties when violations are detected.

NOTES

[1] Because of concerns over "interviewer effects," that is, interviewer attitudes or behavior influencing survey responses, a double-blind interviewing procedure was utilized. Neither the interviewers nor the establishments knew of the study's interest in illegal aliens or the specific lists from which the employer names and addresses were selected.

[2] Distribution of years of operation of the establishment (percent):

Sample	Less than 2 years	2-5years	5-10 years	10 or more years	Total (number)
INS Sample	2.1	12.4	14.0	71.5	100.0 (193)
General Sample	2.8	10.3	14.1	72.8	100.0 (213)
All	2.5	11.3	14.0	72.2	100.0 (406)

[3] When the dependent variable ILLEMP is unity for the INS sample employers and zero for the general sample, the coefficients and t-ratios are:

	Coefficient	T-ratio
Size	0.0016	7.25
Size squared	-0.0006×10^{-3}	-5.77
Age	0.3683	2.37
Age squared	-0.0390	-2.72
Const.	-0.3821	-0.94

$R^2 = 0.13$
$N = 406$

Mean age of establishments is 6.05 years.

4 Distribution by subindustry within manufacturing (percent):

Sample	Durable Manuf.	Nondurable Manuf.	Const.	Total	Number
INS Sample	59.5	36.5	4.1	100.0	74
General Sample	54.6	29.9	15.5	100.0	97
All	56.7	32.7	10.5	100.0	171

5 Distribution by subindustry and nationality within Other Services (percent):

Sample	Land-scaping	Retail Trade	Business and Repair	Finance Ins., R.E.	Health Prof.
INS Sample	27.4	22.5	9.7	0.0	11.3
Mexican	42.1	23.7	5.3	0.0	2.6
Non-Mexican	4.2	20.8	16.7	0.0	25.0
General Sample	6.6	38.2	21.1	17.1	3.9
All	15.9	31.2	15.9	9.4	7.2

Sample	Other Prof.	Personal Services	Transp. and Utilities	Entertain. & Recreat.	Total	Number
INS Sample	0.0	14.5	8.1	6.5	100.0	62
Mexican	0.0	18.4	0.0	7.9	100.0	38
Non-Mexican	0.0	8.3	20.8	4.2	100.0	24
General Sample	5.3	2.6	5.3	0.0	100.0	76
All	2.9	8.0	6.5	2.9	100.0	138

6 An establishment is coded as owned by an Hispanic if one or more of the owners, partners or family corporation stockholders is Hispanic. There were virtually no Asian owners in the sample. Many Asian-owned businesses have fewer than five employees and hence would not be eligible for inclusion in the survey.

7 The data under study are not suitable for testing the hypothesis that the establishments in the INS sample have fewer employees. Because of the sampling procedure, the probability that an establishment is in the INS sample is greater the larger the number of its employees, while the probability that an establishment is in the general sample is virtually independent of the number of employees. Thus, the sampling procedures bias the sample in favor of larger employers of illegal aliens. The variable for size is included in the analysis, in a quadratic form, to control statistically for the effects of this feature of the sampling methodology. The coefficients of the other explanatory variables in the regression analysis measure partial effects when the number of employees is held constant.

8 This is not surprising. Pindyck and Rubinfeld (1981, p. 278-279) show that when the average value of a dichotomous dependent variable is around 0.5, as it is in this study, OLS tends to give results which are very similar to logit.

[9] It is not known whether the illegal alien is a union member.

[10] A franchise was classified as independently owned or a branch/subsidiary depending on whether the holder of the franchise was an independent operator or a firm that owned or controlled more than one establishment.

[11] Partial effect of seasonality on whether the employer is from the illegal alien sample (ILLEMP), by industry:[a]

On Season[b]	All	Manufacturing	Restaurants	Other Service
Spring	-0.022	-0.074	-0.123	0.095
	(-0.269)	(-0.585)	(-0.380)	(0.902)
Summer	0.074	-0.028	0.106	0.061
	(1.054)	(-0.269)	(0.579)	(0.509)
Winter	-0.154	0.017	0.258	-0.127
	(-0.228)	(0.171)	(0.644)	(-1.463)
Fall	-0.195	0.055	-0.158	-0.369
	(-2.542)	(0.463)	(-0.542)	(-3.354)
Number of Observations	399	165	96	138

a. Controlling for size, degree of unionization, type of ownership, ethnicity of owner, and proportion of Hispanics and Asians in the workforce. Entries are OLS regression coefficients with t-ratios in parentheses.

b. The "on season" dichotomous variable is unity if the employer reported no seasonality or if the employer reported that two of the three months in the quarter are months of high employment.

[12] The proportion of owners classified as Hispanic is 6.3 percent for restaurants, 1.8 percent for manufacturing, 1.4 percent for other services, and 2.8 percent overall.

[13] This could arise even if INS did not target employer raids on larger establishments that employ illegal aliens.

[14] The 1986 Immigration Reform and Control Act makes it illegal for an employer to knowingly hire illegal aliens and requires employers to check although not validate the authenticity of certain documents to ascertain the job applicant's legal status. The legislation is likely to increase the size of the underground economy. Enforcement of the employer sections provisions will be difficult, and will be particularly difficult against employers who also violate payroll tax and income tax withholding requirements.

[15] Form of payment by industry and type of employer:

	INS Sample		General Sample		Total	
	All Industries	Restaurants	All Industries	Restaurants	All Industries	Restaurants
Cash[a]	7[c]	5	6	6	13	11
Check[b]	185	52	204	34	389	86
Total	192	57	210	40	402	97

a. Payment of part or all of wages in cash.

b. Includes checks, vouchers and direct deposit.

c. Includes one establishment in other services and one in manufacturing.

Although 9 percent of the INS sample and 15 percent of the general sample of restaurants reported cash payments, the difference disappears when restaurant size is held constant.

[16] Distribution of employers by the proportion of new hires required to have a social security number, by industry and sample:

Percent of Hires	Manufacturing		Restaurant		Other Service		All Industries	
	INS Sample	General Sample	INS Sample	General Sample	INS Sample	General Sample	INS Sample	General Sample
0	2	1	0	0	1	0	3	1
1-19	0	1	0	0	0	0	0	1
20-39	1	0	0	0	0	1	1	1
40-59	1	0	0	0	0	0	1	0
60-79	0	0	0	0	0	0	0	0
80-99	0	0	1	1	0	0	1	1
100	67	85	52	37	59	65	178	187
Total	71	87	53	38	60	66	184	191

[17] The means, standard deviations, regression coefficients, and t-ratios are:

Variable	Mean	S.D.	Sample Size	Training Variable Regression Coefficient[a] (t-ratio)	Training Variable Regression Coefficient[b] (t-ratio)
TRNOPRIOR[c]	155.8	258.3	365	-0.00028 (-2.95)	-0.00013 (-1.28)
TRYESPRIOR[c]	45.3	97.2	386	-0.00089 (-3.62)	-0.00054 (-2.23)

a. Dependent variable is ILLEMP, also controlling for SIZE and SIZESQ.

b. Dependent variable is ILLEMP, also controlling for SIZE, SIZESQ, and the occupation of the most common male nonsupervisory job.

c. Business days of training if the worker had no prior experience (TRNOPRIOR) and if the worker had prior experience (TRYESPRIOR) in the job. Four separate regressions are estimated.

[18] The Immigration Reform and Control Act of 1986 makes this form of discrimination illegal.

[19] The response rate ("yes" or "no" responses as a proportion of the sample) was lowest for this question, 83 percent. For all other questions on hiring requirements it ranged from about 90 percent to 97 percent.

6

The Labor Market and Public Policy

This book has analyzed the employment and employers of illegal aliens in an urban labor market. By concentrating on the Chicago labor market, it could analyze employment in a diverse set of sectors for illegal aliens from Mexico and other countries of origin. The immediate purpose of the study was to increase substantially the conceptual and empirical knowledge regarding the labor market adjustment of illegal aliens and hence their impact on the U.S. economy. This also sheds light on the broader issues of the adjustment and impact of legal immigrants and the functioning of the U.S. labor market. The study uses unique matched employee-employer data on illegal aliens. In spite of recent developments in labor market data, matched employee-employer data are still very rare.

The analyses reported in the previous chapters have implications for survey research methodology, understanding the illegal alien labor market, and the likely impacts of the Immigration Reform and Control Act of 1986.

I. The Setting

The illegal alien labor market is discussed in chapter 2. Illegal immigration arises from a divergence between the economic and other incentives for international migration and the migration that is permitted by U.S. immigration law. Both issues were discussed. Among those who cannot migrate legally in spite of their wishes to do so, only some choose to become illegal aliens. Illegal aliens tend to be low-skilled young adult workers unaccompanied by dependent family members from low-income countries with close proximity to the U.S.

It has been estimated that in 1980 there were 3.5 to 6.0 million illegal aliens in the U.S., of whom about half were Mexican nationals. Their number has increased since then. Illegal aliens have a high labor force participation rate, and by 1986 there may have been as many as 4 million in the U.S. labor market, or about 4 percent of the labor force.

The Immigration Reform and Control Act of 1986 was enacted as a result of the obvious inability of the then-current policy to stem the flow of illegal aliens. The legislation introduced penalties against employers who knowingly hire illegal aliens and offered amnesty to illegal aliens who resided continuously in the U.S since before January 1982. It is not likely that the 1986 Act will end illegal immigration since the incentives are still so strong. It will take some time before the implications of the Act's provisions are well understood.[1]

II. Survey Methodology

The survey procedures were developed and analyzed in chapter 3. The analysis is based on two data sets that are partially merged. One data set is a sample of employed male illegal aliens randomly selected from the population of illegal aliens apprehended in 1983 by the Chicago District Office of the Immigration and Naturalization Service (INS). Data on the demographic and labor market characteristics of the illegal aliens were successfully abstracted and coded from the Record of Deportable Alien, INS form I-213. Non-Mexican illegal aliens were oversampled relative to those of Mexican origin to provide a sufficiently large sample for statistical analysis.

The illegal aliens' responses to the I-213 question on the name and address of their current or most recent employer generated a sample of establishments that have employed illegal aliens. Another sample was randomly selected from industry directories, matched by major industry category—manufacturing, restaurant, and other services. A double-blind survey procedure was employed in that neither the respondent at the establishment nor the interviewer knew that half of the sample was drawn from information provided by illegal aliens. The respondent was the person in charge of hiring workers for the most common male nonsupervisory job.

This unique survey methodology was very successful. The most conservative measure of the completion rate for the employer survey is the number of completed interviews as a percent of all sample cases not known to be ineligible. The rate was 77 percent overall; 76 percent for the establishments identified in the INS files and 79 percent in the general sample. There was a low incidence, with little difference between the two sample sources, of either partial interviews or item nonresponse. Indeed, the establishment respondents seemed generally eager to participate.

The success of the survey research methodology should be encouraging to those whose research questions require matched employee-employer data. There is nothing in the methodology that would suggest that the success was limited to the particular characteristics of the Chicago metropolitan area or of the illegal alien labor market. Since so many labor market research studies require matched employee-employer data to properly test their hypotheses, this project offers hope for future progress in this area

III. The Illegal Alien Labor Market

The analysis of the illegal alien labor market produces many rich and robust findings.

When the illegal alien is treated as the unit of observation, as in chapter 4, it is possible to study wage determination, job mobility, and employer exploitation, among other issues. The analysis of wages shows that the illegal alien's skills clearly matter. Aliens with more labor market experience in the home country, with more experience in the U.S., and with a longer job tenure with their current (or recent) U.S. employer have higher wages, with the effect of the experience being greater the more closely it relates to their current employment. The wages of illegal aliens are also higher if they work for more "desirable" employers. These include establishments that are unionized, pay higher wages for the same formal level of skill, and have a more highly skilled workforce.

Illegal aliens who entered the U.S. with student visas seem to have lower wages, possibly because combining schooling with labor market activities constrains the set of available job opportunities. The restaurant sector appears to offer lower money wages than either manufacturing or other services, but the value of free meals and tip income may not have been included in the wages reported by the aliens.

The illegal aliens exhibit considerable job mobility. Those who have been in the U.S. for a longer period of time have presumably acquired more knowledge and skills relevant for the U.S. labor market. It is found that they are more likely to be working in the higher paid manufacturing sector, and to be working for a larger, more highly unionized establishment that has a higher wage structure (if worker skills are held constant) and a more highly skilled workforce. The European and Canadian illegal aliens are more likely to work for the most desirable establishments.

Mexican illegal aliens display employment characteristics that would be associated with temporary migrants. They are more likely to work for establishments with seasonal employment patterns. Among all the illegal aliens, those of Mexican origin experience the lowest cost of to-and-fro migration, and the lowest cost of attempting another re-entry if apprehended at the border. Seasonal employment may dovetail nicely with the Mexican illegal aliens' preference for jobs that permit long visits to their families in Mexico.

The Mexican illegal aliens, much more than others, also exhibit ethnic enclave patterns of employment. Ethnic-enclave employment requires fewer U.S.-specific skills and is therefore better suited to a temporary migrant population for which large destination-specific human capital investments would not be cost-effective. It is facilitated by the very large Mexican or Hispanic community in Chicago, which can sustain substantial ethnic enclave employment. While easing an initial or temporary adjustment to the U.S labor market, ethnic enclave employment may retard the subsequent "Americanization" of their skills.

The extent to which illegal aliens are "exploited" by employers has been a subject of lively debate. To some, exploitation means the payment of wages below the legal minimum. This study indicates that the payment of below-minimum wage rates to illegal aliens is rare and is more common in the restaurant sector. It should be noted, however, that the value of free meals and tips may not have been included in the reported wages for workers in the restaurant sector and that a lower legal minimum is applicable in this sector. In addition, below-minimum wages are associated with recency of arrival in the U.S. Thus, to the extent that wage payments below the legal minimum level exist, they appear to be a temporary experience.

To some, exploitation means that workers are locked into dead-end jobs. The analysis suggests, however, that the substantial wage increases with U.S. experience, particularly experience with their current employer, is inconsistent with the dead-end job hypothesis. Furthermore, the illegal aliens experience considerable job mobility, moving on to more attractive jobs as they acquire U.S. labor market experience. They undergo favorable job mobility even if they remain in an ethnic enclave.

There is no denying that illegal aliens are paid low wages relative to the average U.S. worker. But the low wages of illegal aliens do not appear to be the result of employer exploitation. Rather, they appear to be the result of low skill levels. Most illegal aliens have low levels of schooling, limited fluency in English, and are relative newcomers in the U.S. labor market. In addition, the skill differential is in part a consequence of the lower incentives for the illegal aliens and their employers for making job-training investments that are specific to the U.S. labor market or their U.S. employer. These lower incentives may be a consequence of the realistic expectation of a higher probability of return migration, that is, the perceived temporary nature of much of the illegal migration.

The establishments known to have employed illegal aliens are compared with the randomly selected establishments in chapter 5. The general sample includes some establishments that have employed illegal aliens. As a result, this analysis biases downward the magnitude of the true differences between employers of illegal aliens and establishments that do not employ them.

The salient differences between the establishments identified by the apprehended illegal aliens and the general sample of establishments appear to be that the former concentrate on the employment of low-skilled, minority workers and are better suited for the employment of temporary workers. The occupational skill level of the employees in the INS sample of establishments is considerably lower than in the general sample. Their workers also receive less on-the-job training from the firm. In particular, the differences in training opportunities are most pronounced for firm-specific training, that is, training that is useful only in the firm in which it is acquired.

Seasonal patterns of employment are more common among the employers of illegal aliens, and their "off season" tends to be longer. They also exhibit more ethnic enclave characteristics. In the INS sample, a larger proportion of the workforce is of Hispanic or Asian origin; in manufacturing, the owner is more likely to be an Hispanic.

Some other characteristics sometimes said to be distinguishing features of employers of illegal aliens do not appear to matter. The illegal alien employers in this study are not more likely than the general sample employers to be part of the underground economy. In addition, there is no clear relation between the age of the establishment—that is, how long it has been in business—and whether it is an employer of illegal aliens.

The analysis indicates that the illegal aliens have adapted very well to the U.S. labor market. Although there is some industrial, occupational and ethnic concentration, these appear to be optimal responses to their skills, fluency in English, knowledge of the U.S. labor market, proximity to the country of origin, and the temporary nature of much of their migration. It would be inappropriate to characterize illegal aliens as forming a separate subeconomy, as doing jobs that others either do not do or would not do, or as a noncompeting group in the labor market.

IV. The Impact of the Immigration Reform and Control Act

This study has several implications for the likely consequences of the Immigration Reform and Control Act of 1986 on the illegal alien labor market.

The 1986 Act introduces " employer sanctions," that is, penalties against employers who knowingly hire illegal aliens. The analysis suggest, however, that at most establishments in 1984 the person in charge of hiring believed that this was already the law of the land. There was little difference in response between the employers identified by an apprehended illegal alien and those randomly selected from directories. This means that the "announcement effect" of the new legislation for deterring the hiring of illegal aliens is likely to be minimal. For the legislation to have a significant impact, substantial resources may have to be devoted to enforcement, and meaningful penalties will have to be imposed. Considering the minimal level of enforcement resources appropriated in the past for immigration control, particularly enforcement away from the border, one may be justifiable skeptical about future appropriations.

The analysis has identified characteristics of establishments that are more likely to be hiring illegal aliens. This profile can be used to enhance the target efficiency of the resources devoted to enforcing employer sanctions. On the other hand, the findings also suggest that the employment of illegal aliens is widespread in the low-skilled labor market, even though there are pockets of concentration. The widespread nature of illegal alien employment will make enforcement more difficult.

It is expected that if there is stringent enforcement of employer sanctions, job opportunities and hence wage offers for illegal aliens will decrease. The new law includes a " grandfather clause," that is, only new hires need to be tested for their legal status, not all currently employed workers. This means that illegal aliens who do not qualify for or who do not apply for legalization will have greater difficulty finding another job. Future flows of illegal aliens will also find their job mobility reduced. As a result of reducing the most effective instrument against employer exploitation, job mobility, it should be expected that the incidence of employer exploitation, in the form of wages below the legal minimum level and undesirable working conditions, will increase in the future.

Over 2¼ million illegal aliens have acquired legal rights to live and work in the United States as a direct result of the amnesty offered in the 1986 Act. After a period of time, these now-legalized aliens will also be able to sponsor the legal migration of immediate family members who have remained in the country of origin or are in the U.S. in an illegal status. If so seasonal migration is likely to decline and the attachment of the now-legalized aliens to the U.S. labor market is likely to increase. It can be expected that as their permanent attachment to the U.S. labor market increases, these workers will have a greater incentive for making job training investments that are more specific to the U.S. labor market and their U.S. employers. Their employers will be similarly inclined. The likely consequence is greater job training and enhanced occupational and income mobility for the legalized aliens. They are, however, likely to remain relatively low-skilled workers because of their low educational attainment.

If the deterrent affect of employer sanctions on new illegal migration is not sufficiently strong, wage opportunities in the low-skilled labor market may decrease. This may arise for several reasons. First, the legalized aliens are now likely to have a greater attachment to the U.S. labor market, reducing both season and permanent return migration. This implifies a greater supply of labor to the low-skilled labor market. Second, some, and perhaps many, of the dependent family members whose immigration is sponsored by the now-legalized aliens will enter the labor force. If these are predominantly low-skilled workers, perhaps disproportionately female, the supply of low-skilled workers will expand even further. Third, to the extent that employer sanctions are enforced, employers will have to verify the legal status of each worker hired. The verification process is not without cost. In effect, employer sanctions are the equivalent of a "hiring tax." Relative to wage rates, the "hiring tax" is more burdensome for low-wage workers in part-time, high turnover, or seasonal jobs. This will reduce the demand for workers in the low-wage, low-skilled labor market.

While the intended direct effect of employer sanctions is to raise wages in the low-skilled labor market for workers with legal rights to work in this country, the indirect effects have the opposite impact. The net impact cannot be determined *a priori,* and it may take several years for the direct and indirect effects to work their way through the economic system. Only then may there be a degree of certainty as to the net effect of the legislation on wages and job opportunities for low-skilled workers.

NOTES

[1] For a discussion of the provisions of the 1986 Act, and an analysis of its implications for illegal immigration and the labor market see Chiswick (1988).

Bibliography

Ashenfelter, Orley and Smith, Roberts S. (1979), "Compliance with the Minimum Wage Law," *Journal of Political Economy,* April, pp. 333-350.

Bailey, Thomas (1985), "A Case Study of Immigrants in the Restaurant Industry," *Industrial Relations,* Spring, pp. 205-221.

Barron, John M., Dan A. Block and Mark A. Loewenstein (1987), "Employer Size: The Implications for Search, Training, Capital Investment, Starting Wages and Wage Growth," *Journal of Labor Economics,* January, pp. 76-89.

Bustamante, Jorge A. (1977), "Undocumented Immigration from Mexico: Research Report," *International Migration Review,* Summer, pp. 149-177.

Cafferty, Pastora San Juan, Barry R. Chiswick, Andrew M. Greeley and Teresa A. Sullivan (1983), *The Dilemma of American Immigration: Beyond the Golden Door,* New Brunswick: Transaction Books.

Cardenas, Gilbert (1979), "Mexican Illegal Aliens in the San Antonio Labor Market," *Texas Business Review,* November, pp. 187-191.

Carliner, David (1977), *The Rights of Aliens: The Basic ACLU Guide to an Alien's Rights,* New York: Avon Books.

Chiswick, Barry A. (1979), "The Economic Progress of Immigrants: Some Apparently Universal Patterns," in William Fellner, editor, *Contemporary Economic Problems, 1979,* Washington: American Enterprise Institute, pp. 359-399.

_____. (1984), "Illegal Aliens in the United States Labor Market: Analysis of Occupational Attainment and Earnings," *International Migration Review,* Fall, pp. 714-732.

_____. (1985), *The Employment and Employers of Illegal Aliens: The Survey and Analysis of Data,* Vol. I and Vol. II, University of Illinois at Chicago, July, mimeo.

149

_____. (1986a), "Illegal Aliens: A Preliminary Report on an Employee-Employer Survey," *American Economic Review,* May, pp. 253-257.

_____. (1986b), "The Illegal Alien Policy Dilemma" in Susan Pozo, ed., *Essays on Legal and Illegal Immigration,* Kalamazoo: W. E. Upjohn Institute for Employment Research, pp. 73-87.

_____. (1988) "Illegal Immigration and Immigration Control," *Journal of Economic Perspectives* (August).

_____. and Francis Fullam (1980), "A Feasibility Study for a Survey of the employers of Undocumented Aliens: Project Report." Report prepared for Employment and Training Administration, U.S. Department of Labor, June (N.T.I.S. No. PB80-208879).

Cornelius, Wayne (1976), "Mexican Migration to the United States: The View from Rural Sending Communities," Migration and Development Study Group, Working Paper Series, M.I.T., June, mimeo.

Cross, Harry E. and James A. Sandos (1981), *Across the Border: Rural Development in Mexico and Recent Migration to the United States,* Berkeley: University of California Press.

Cuthbert, Richard W. and Joe B. Stevens (1981), "The Net Economic Incentive for Illegal Mexican Migration: A Case Study," *International Migration Review,* Fall, pp. 543-550.

Davidson, Christine A. (1981), "Characteristics of Deportable Aliens Located in the Interior of the United States," Paper presented at Annual Meetings, Population Association of America, mimeo.

Diez-Canedo, Juan (1980), "A New View of Mexican Migration to the United States," Ph.D. Dissertation, Massachusetts Institute of Technology.

Freeman, Richard (1984), "Longitudinal Analysis of the Effects of Trade Unions," *Journal of Labor Economics,* January, pp. 1-26.

Huddle, Donald L., Arthur F. Corwin and Gerald J. MacDonald (1985), *Illegal Immigration: Job Displacement and Social Cost,* American Immigration and Control Foundation, Alexandria, Va.

International Migration Review (1984), Special Issue, *Irregular Migration: An International Perspective,* Fall.

Immigration Statistics: A Story of Neglect (1985), Washington: National Research Council.

Keely, Charles (1982), "Illegal Migration," *Scientific American,* March, pp. 41-47.

Kossoudji, Sherrie A. and Susan I. Ranney (1984), "Wage Rates of Temporary Mexican Migrants to the U.S.: The Role of Legal Status," Paper presented at the Econometric Society Annual Meetings, Dallas, December.

Lazear, Edward, (1977), "Schooling as a Wage Depressant," *Journal of Human Resources,* Spring, pp. 164-176.

Lewis, H. Gregg (1983), "Union Relative Wage Effects: A Survey of Macro Estimates," *Journal of Labor Economics,* January, pp. 1-27.

Martin, Philip L. and Ellen B. Sehgal (1980), "Illegal Immigration: The Guestworker Option," *Public Policy,* Spring, pp. 20-29.

Massey, Douglas S. (1987), "Do Undocumented Migrants Earn Lower Wages than Legal Immigrants? New Evidence from Mexico," *International Migration Review,* (Summer), pp. 236-274.

Mellow, Wesley (1982), "Employer Size and Wages," *Review of Economics and Statistics,* August, pp. 495-501.

North, David S. (1981), "Government Records: What They Tell Us about the Role of Illegal Aliens in the Labor Market and in Income Transfer Programs," New Transcentury Foundation, April, mimeo.

_____. and Marion F. Houstoun (1976), *The Characteristics and Role of Illegal Aliens in the United States Labor Market: An Exploratory Study,* Washington, Linton and Co.

Papandemetriou, Demetrios G. and Nicholas DiMarzio (1986), *Undocumented Aliens in the New York Metropolitan Area,* Staten Island, NY: Center for Migration Studies.

Passel, Jeffrey S. and Karen A. Woodrow (1984), "Geographic Distribution of Undocumented Immigrants: Estimates of Undocumented Aliens Counted in the 1980 Census by State," *International Migration Review,* Fall, pp. 642-671.

Pindyck, Robert S. and Daniel L. Rubinfeld (1981), *Econometric Models and Economic Forecasts,* New York: McGraw Hill, 2nd ed.

Piore, Michael (1979), *Birds of Passage: Migrant Labor and Industrial Society,* Cambridge: Cambridge University Press.

Portes, Alejandro (1977), "Labor Functions of Illegal Aliens," *Society,* October, pp. 31-37.

Ranney, Susan and Sherrie Kossoudji (1983), "Profiles of Temporary Mexican Labor Migrants to the United States," *Population and Development Review* (September), pp. 475-93.

Rees, Albert and George P. Shultz (1970), *Workers and Wages in an Urban Labor Market,* Chicago, University of Chicago Press.

Select Commission on Immigration and Refugee Policy (1981a), *U.S. Immigration Policy and the National Interest,* Washington: U.S. Government Printing Office.

Select Commission on Immigration and Refugee Policy (1981b), "Current Laws Inhibiting the Employment of Undocumented Aliens in the

152

United States," in SCIRP, *U.S. Immigration Policy and the National Interest*, Appendix E, *Papers on Illegal Migration to the United States*, Washington: U.S. Government Printing Office.

Siegal, Jacob S., Jeffrey S. Passel and J. Gregory Robinson (1981), "Preliminary Review of Existing Studies of the Number of Illegal Residents of the United States," in Select Commission on Immigration and Refugee Policy, *U.S. Immigration Policy and the National Interest*, Appendix E, *Papers on Illegal Migration to the United States*, Washington, pp. 13-40.

Simon, Carl P. and Ann D. Witte (1982), *Beating the System: the Underground Economy*, Boston: Auburn House.

Simon Rita J. and Margo DeLey (1984), "The Work Experience of Undocumented Mexican Women Migrants in Los Angeles," *International Migration Review*, Winter, pp. 1212-1229.

U.S. Department of Justice (1976), *Preliminary Report, Domestic Council Committee on Illegal Aliens*, Washington: U.S. Department of Justice.

U.S. Department of Justice, Immigration and Naturalization Service (1979), *Immigration Literature: Abstracts of Demographic, Economic and Policy Studies*, Washington: U.S. Department of Justice.

U.S. Department of Justice, Immigration and Naturalization Service (various years) *Statistical Yearbook of the Immigration and Naturalization Service*. Washington: U.S. Department of Justice.

U.S. House of Representatives (1986), *Immigration Reform and Control Act of 1986-Conference Report*, Report 99-100, October 14, 1986.

Van Arsdol, Maurice, et al. (1978), *Non-Apprehended and Apprehended Illegal Residents in the Los Angeles Labor Market: An Exploratory Study*, Los Angeles: University of Southern California, mimeo.

Exhibit 1
Record of Deportable Alien (I-213) Form

RECORD OF DEPORTABLE ALIEN (See A.M. – 2790.31-.34 for Instructions)

Family Name (Capital Letters)	Given Name	Middle Name		Sex	Hair	Eyes	Complexion
Country of Citizenship	Passport Number and Country of Issue	File Number		Height	Weight	Occupation	
U.S. Address (Residence) (Number) (Street) (City) (State) (Zip Code)				Scars or Marks			
Date, Place, Time, Manner of Last Entry		Passenger Boarded At		F.B.I. No.	Marital Status ☐ Single ☐ Separated	☐ Widow(er) ☐ Married ☐ Divorced	
Number, Street, City, Province (State) and Country of Permanent Residence				Method of Location/Apprehension			
Birthdate	Date of Action	Location Code		(At/Near)	Date & Hour		
City, Province (State) and Country of Birth	AR Form: (Type & No.) ☐ ☐	☐ Lifted ☐ Not Lifted		By			
Visa Issued At – NIV No.	Social Security Account Name			Status at Entry	Status When Found		
Date Visa Issued	Social Security No.	Send C.O. Rec. Check To:		Length of Time Illegally in U.S.			
Immigration Record		Criminal Record					
Name, Address, and Nationality of Spouse (Maiden Name, if appropriate)				Number & Nationality of Minor Children			
Father's Name, and Nationality and Address, if Known		Mother's Present and Maiden Names, Nationality, and Address, if Known					
Monies Due/Property in U.S. Not in Immediate Possession ☐ None Claimed ☐ See Form I-43	Fingerprinted ☐ Yes ☐ No	Lookout Book Checked ☐ Not Listed ☐ Listed, Code ____		Deportation Charge(s) (Code Words)			
Name and Address of (Last) (Current) U.S. Employer	Type of Employment	Salary $ ____ hr.		From:	To:		

PLEASE TYPEWRITE OR PRINT IN BLOCK CAPITAL LETTERS

Narrative (Outline particulars under which alien located/apprehended. Include details, not shown above, re time, place, manner of last entry, and elements which establish administrative and/or criminal violation. Indicate means and route of travel to interior.) Alien has been advised of communication privileges pursuant to 8 CFR 242.2(e).
Initial _____ Date _____

(If space insufficient, show "continued" and continue on reverse, from bottom up):   (Signature and Title)

DISTRIBUTION	Received (subject and documents) (report of interview) from
	Officer: _____
	_____ 19____ at _____ ( ). ____ M.
	Disposition _____
	(Receiving Officer) _____

Form I-213 (Rev. 4-16-79)Y UNITED STATES DEPARTMENT OF JUSTICE Immigration and Naturalization Service

153

Exhibit 2
Types of Questions in Employer Survey .

1. *Business Organization*—Type of ownership, industry, major product or service, age of establishment. Volume of sales, race/ethnicity of ower(s) (if not a corporation) and manager of establishment. Characteristics of respondent (person in charge of hiring workers for the most common male non-supervisory job).

2. *Hiring Practices*—Number of workers hired in past years, sources of these hires (union hiring hall, employment agencies, references from employees, walk-ins, etc.), requirements at hiring (includes work experience, references, knowledge of English, social security number, citizenship or green card, union membership, etc.).

3. *Current Employees*—Number of employees by sex, race/ethnicity and full-time/part-time status. Educational attainment.

4. *Characteristics of Compensation*—Wage rates overall and by experience and education, seasonality of employment, unionization, on-the-job training, frequency and method of payment.

5. *Older Workers, Teenagers, Adult Men, Adult Women, Recent Immigrants*—(Parallel questions for each group). Number of employees and recent hires by sex and race/ethnicity. Number who left and reasons for leaving. Questions for recent immigrants (i.e., persons who came to the U.S. to stay within the past 5 years), include citizenship/visa status, country of origin and, among reasons for leaving establishment, apprehension by INS.

6. *Understanding of Labor Legislation*—Questions regarding understanding of legal status of various hiring practices regarding women, the handicapped, the aged, union members and immigrants.

NOTE: The employer questionnaire is reproduced in Chiswick, (1985, Volume II.)

Index